Family Circle. ABZ's of Cooking

Edited by Lucy Wing with
The Family Circle Food Department

Volume 8

Introduction

Variety is the spice of life and that's what this volume is all about. We have included recipes for economical and nutritious navy beans, a luscious nectarine salad and desserts plus tasty international noodle recipes.

Under oats, you'll find the ever-popular oatmeal raisin cookie in addition to bar cookies, griddle cakes and spicy oatmeal served with ice cream instead of milk. Under olives, we have included information on the different types available plus some mouth-watering recipes. For omelets, you'll find savory and sweet ones, all quick and easy to prepare. Onions are used to add special flavor to other dishes and they can also be served as an appetizer when pickled, as a main dish when stuffed with a meat filling, or even as a salad. Look in our orange section for zesty main dishes, accompaniments and desserts. Use our oyster recipes to make succulent appetizers, soup or sandwiches.

Many food topics are found under the letter "P." Among them is pasta, an inexpensive standby for quick and delicious meals. You'll find pastry recipes using a homemade dough or a frozen, convenient product sold in the supermarket. Peas, peaches, peanuts, pears, peppercorns, picnic foods, pie—both main dish and dessert—plus pineapple and pizza, all add up to variety and wonderful eating.

Contents

Cover photo: Spaghetti with Meat Sauce, page 480

ISBN 0-8249-9008-0

Published by Ideals Publishing Corporation
11315 Watertown Plank Road
Milwaukee, WI 53226

Family Circle Staff

Project Editor	Lucy Wing
Food Editor	Jean Hewitt
Senior Associate Food Editor	Jane O'Keefe
Art Director	Joseph Taveroni
Copy Editor	Susan Tierney
Project Management	Annabelle Arenz
	John Jaxheimer

Ideals Publishing Staff

Project Editor	Julie Hogan
Food Stylist	Susan Noland
Photographer	Gerald Koser
Project Management	James Kuse
	Marybeth Owens

Photographs by: Avedis, Paul Christensen, Richard
Jeffery, Allen Lieberman, Bill McGinn, Rudy Muller, George
Nordhausen, Gordon E. Smith, Bob Stoller, Rene Velez

NACHO A Mexican snack consisting of a triangular piece of crisply fried corn tortilla topped with cheese and chile pepper. Nachos are served as a Tex-Mex appetizer.

NACHOS

Bake at 350° for 5 minutes.
Makes 24 nachos or 6 to 8 servings.

- **6 fresh or frozen and thawed corn tortillas**
  Vegetable oil for frying
  Salt
- **1 can (3½ ounces) hot jalapeño chile peppers**
  OR: **1 can (4 ounces) whole mild green chilies**
- **1 cup refried beans**
- **2 ounces longhorn, mild Cheddar or Monterey Jack cheese, shredded (½ cup)**

1. Cut tortillas into quarters to form triangular-shaped wedges. Heat about ⅛ inch oil in skillet until hot. Sauté a few at a time, turning occasionally, until crisp and golden brown. Drain on paper toweling. Sprinkle lightly with salt. Preheat oven to 350°.
2. Drain chile peppers or chilies; remove seeds or stem and pith. Cut into ¼-inch strips. Spread each tortilla chip with beans, sprinkle with cheese and top with chile strip. Place nachos on cookie sheet.

3. Bake in a preheated moderate oven (350°) for 5 minutes or until beans are hot and cheese melts. Serve immediately.

● ● ●

NAVY BEANS These small, firm, dried white beans are used extensively commercially for pork and beans, and beans in tomato sauce. They are related to and often used interchangeably with pea beans. Pea beans are the smallest of the white beans. Both varieties of beans keep their shape under long, slow cooking. These beans are the most versatile of the dried beans, equally suited to soups, salads and casseroles. They're the beans made famous in old-fashioned Boston Baked Beans. See also **BEANS.**

BEAN AND SAUSAGE SOUP

Makes 8 servings.

- **1 pound dried navy beans**
- **8 cups water**
- **1 bay leaf**
- **1 large onion**
- **1 whole clove**
- **1¼ teaspoons salt**
- **3 tablespoons butter or margarine**
- **2 medium-size onions, minced (1 cup)**
- **2 carrots, minced**
- **1 cup minced celery**
- **2 tablespoons tomato paste**
- **4 cans (13¾ ounces each) beef broth**
- **½ teaspoon pepper**
- **½ cup broken thin spaghetti**
- **3 frankfurters, thinly sliced**
- **2 tablespoons minced fresh parsley**
- **1 clove garlic, minced**

1. Pick over beans; rinse under running water. Combine with water in a large kettle or Dutch oven. Add bay leaf, onion, clove and ¼ teaspoon of the salt. Bring to boiling; cover. Boil 2 minutes; remove from heat; let stand 1 hour.
2. Return to heat. Bring to boiling; lower heat. Simmer 2 hours or until beans are tender; drain.
3. Heat the butter in a large flame-proof casserole or Dutch oven. Cook onions, carrots and celery over low heat until soft but not brown.
4. Add tomato paste, 3 cups of the cooked beans, broth, remaining 1 teaspoon salt and the pepper. Bring to boiling; lower heat. Simmer, covered, 40 minutes. Puree remaining beans; reserve.
5. Add the spaghetti to the soup; cook for 10 minutes or until spaghetti is tender.
6. Add the bean puree and frankfurters; heat through. Taste; add additional seasoning, if you wish.
7. Combine parsley and garlic and sprinkle over soup.

MAPLE BAKED BEANS WITH BACON

This tasty treat is lightly glazed, sweet and spicy beans.

Bake at 325° for 2 hours.
Makes about 6 servings.

 1 **pound dried navy or pea beans**
 7 **cups water**
 ½ **pound lean slab bacon**
 1 **medium-size onion, chopped (½ cup)**
1½ **teaspoons salt**
 1 **teaspoon ground ginger**
 ½ **teaspoon ground allspice**
 ¼ **teaspoon pepper**
 2 **tablespoons cider vinegar**
 ⅔ **cup maple or maple-blended syrup**

1. Pick over beans and rinse under running water. Combine beans and water in a large kettle; cover; let soak overnight. Or, to quick-soak, bring to boiling; boil 2 minutes; remove from heat. Cover and let stand 1 hour.
2. Bring beans to boiling; lower heat; partially cover and simmer 50 to 60 minutes or until beans are almost tender.
3. Remove the rind from the bacon and discard. Cut bacon into ½-inch cubes. Cook in a medium-size skillet until lightly browned. Add onion and cook 2 minutes, stirring often.
4. Drain beans, reserving liquid. There should be 1½ cups liquid; add water if necessary to make that amount. Add liquid to skillet with salt, ginger, allspice, pepper, vinegar and maple syrup. Bring to boiling. Combine beans and bacon mixture in a 2-quart baking dish; cover.
5. Bake in a slow oven (325°) for 1¾ hours; remove cover. Bake 15 minutes longer or until beans are tender and brown on top.

— ●●● —

NECTARINE Often called a fuzzless peach and believed to be a cross between a peach and a plum. Both approaches are inaccurate — a nectarine is a nectarine. The nectarine actually predates the peach and is related to both the rose and almond families. It was a delicacy in ancient China and the Near East long before the birth of Christ. The name is derived from "nectar," the drink of the gods, because of the fruit's delicious flavor.

While some eastern and southern states grow nectarines in small quantities, California produces over 95 percent of the nectarines. The earliest nectarine varieties were small and white-fleshed. Over 85 varieties have been developed, all since the 1940's. Today's nectarine is yellow-fleshed and large in size, bright golden with a bit of red.

Buying and Storing: Tree-ripened nectarines are the best eating quality; however, they are too delicate to transport to market. They are picked before fully ripe so they are firm enough to transport. Nectarines will be firm to moderately hard but will probably ripen normally within 2 to 3 days at room temperature. Buy bright-looking, plump fruit free of bruises or cracked skins. Fresh nectarines are available from late May to September. Ripe nectarines should be refrigerated until just before use, but for best flavor, return to room temperature before eating.

To Prepare: Nectarines should be thoroughly washed and dried before serving. Peeling the skin isn't necessary. However, if removal is desired, submerge fruit in boiling water for about 30 seconds; remove with a slotted spoon and plunge immediately into cold water. The skin will slip right off. To prevent discoloration after peeling or cutting, dip nectarine into a citrus juice — lemon, orange, lime or grapefruit.

Nectarine Nutrition: A nectarine provides 45 percent of the recommended daily allowance for vitamin A. It is a good source of vitamin C with only 90 calories.

Nectarine Math
1 pound fresh = 3 medium-size = 2½ cups sliced or 2 cups diced

POACHED NECTARINES WITH FLUFFY PASTRY CREAM

Summery fresh nectarines are cooked in lemony syrup just until ten- *der and used to garnish the rich pastry cream.*

Makes 8 servings.

 1 **cup sugar**
1½ **cups ice water**
 8 **large ripe nectarines**
 ½ **cup kirsch or dry white wine**
 1 **small lemon, thinly sliced Fluffy Pastry Cream (recipe follows)**
 1 **tablespoon chopped pistachio nuts**

1. Bring sugar and water to boiling in a large saucepan; boil 5 minutes.
2. Meanwhile, dip nectarines into boiling water 30 seconds, then into ice water 1 minute. Peel, halve and pit nectarines.
3. Add nectarines, kirsch or white wine and lemon slices to sugar syrup. Cover. Cook over low heat, stirring gently, until nectarines are firm but tender, about 10 minutes. Cool; chill.
4. To serve: Drain nectarines. Arrange in a dish around the rim; spoon pastry cream in center; sprinkle with nuts.

FLUFFY PASTRY CREAM

Makes about 2¾ cups.

 ⅓ **cup sugar**
 2 **tablespoons cornstarch**
1½ **teaspoons unflavored gelatin**
 2 **egg yolks**
1½ **cups milk**
 1 **tablespoon butter or margarine**
 1 **teaspoon vanilla**
 ½ **cup heavy cream**

1. Combine sugar, cornstarch and gelatin in a small saucepan. Beat in egg yolks until well mixed. Stir in milk. Cook mixture over low heat, stirring constantly, until thickened, about 10 minutes. Remove from heat.
2. Stir in butter and vanilla. Cover surface with plastic wrap to prevent skin from forming. Chill until cold.
3. Beat cream in small bowl with electric mixer until soft peaks form. Stir chilled custard mixture to soften, then fold in whipped cream until no streaks of white remain.

Pictured opposite: Nectarine and Cucumber Salad, page 454

Nectarine

NECTARINE AND CUCUMBER SALAD

Makes 10 servings.

- 1 container (16 ounces) plain yogurt
- 2 tablespoons chopped fresh mint
- 1 teaspoon salt
- ½ teaspoon sugar
- 1 large clove garlic, minced
- 2½ pounds nectarines, halved, pitted and sliced
  - OR: 1 can (29 ounces) cling peach slices, drained
- 2 cucumbers, pared and thinly sliced

1. Combine yogurt, mint, salt, sugar and garlic in a small bowl.
2. Place a layer of nectarines, then a layer of cucumbers in a shallow serving dish. Spoon some of yogurt mixture over fruits; repeat layering until all are used.
3. Cover and refrigerate for at least 2 hours or overnight, if you wish. Serve with a slotted spoon.

NECTARINE CREAM TORTE

Bake at 350° for 35 minutes.
Makes 8 servings.

- 2 cups *sifted* cake flour
- 2 teaspoons baking powder
- ½ teaspoon salt
- 4 eggs, separated
- 2 cups sugar
- ½ cup (1 stick) butter or margarine
- 1 teaspoon vanilla
- ½ teaspoon almond extract
- ⅓ cup milk
- ¾ cup sliced almonds
- 4 cups sliced, peeled nectarines
- 1 tablespoon lemon juice
- 1 pint heavy cream
- 2 tablespoons 10X (confectioners') sugar

1. Sift flour, baking powder and salt onto wax paper.
2. Beat egg whites in small bowl with electric mixer at high speed until foamy-white and double in volume. Beat in ½ cup of the sugar, 1 tablespoon at a time, until meringue stands in firm peaks. Preheat oven to 350°.
3. Beat 1 cup of the sugar, the butter, egg yolks, vanilla and almond extract in large bowl with electric mixer at high speed for 2 minutes.
4. Stir in flour mixture alternately with milk, beating after each addition, until batter is smooth. Spread batter in two greased and floured 9×9×2-inch pans. Carefully spread meringue over cake batter; sprinkle with all but 2 tablespoons of the sliced almonds.
5. Bake in a preheated moderate oven (350°) for 35 minutes or until meringue is golden brown; remove pans to wire racks to cool. Put reserved 2 tablespoons almonds in a pie plate; bake for 2 minutes; remove.
6. When cake layers are cool enough to handle, loosen around edges with a knife; turn out onto your hand, then gently place, meringue-side up, on wire racks to cool completely.
7. Combine nectarines with lemon juice and ½ cup sugar in a large bowl; let stand 30 minutes; drain and discard syrup.
8. Beat cream with 10X sugar in a bowl; reserve ½ cup. Fold remaining cream into 2 cups fruit.
9. To assemble: Place one cake layer, meringue-side down, on serving plate; spread with nectarine-cream filling; top with remaining cake layer, meringue-side up. Arrange reserved fruit slices and whipped cream on top. Sprinkle with toasted almonds.

● ● ●

NESSELRODE The foods created by the French chef of Count Karl Robert Nesselrode, a Russian count who lived from 1780 to 1862 and loved good eating. The most famous dish created and named in his honor was a dessert using chestnut pieces, candied peel, cherries, raisins and currants flavored with maraschino liqueur and mixed with cream, then frozen in a mold. Today, Nesselrode sauces are commercially bottled containing candied fruits and peel in a heavy syrup. Use them for desserts.

NESSELRODE PIE

Bake at 375° for 8 minutes.
Makes one 9-inch pie.

- 1¼ cups vanilla wafer or shortbread cookie crumbs
- 2 tablespoons sugar (for crust)
- 3 tablespoons butter or margarine, melted
- ¼ cup rum or brandy
- ½ cup mixed candied fruits
- ¼ cup raisins
- 1 jar (10 ounces) marrons (chestnuts) in syrup
- 1 envelope unflavored gelatin
- ¼ cup cold water
- 4 eggs, separated
- ⅔ cup sugar (for filling)
- ¼ teaspoon salt
- ½ cup heavy cream, whipped

1. Preheat oven to 375°. Combine crumbs, the 2 tablespoons sugar and butter in a small bowl; press firmly over bottom and side of a buttered 9-inch pie plate.
2. Bake in a preheated moderate oven (375°) for 8 minutes or until set. Cool completely on wire rack.
3. Pour rum over candied fruits and raisins in a small bowl; let stand 30 minutes. Drain marrons; reserve 3 or 4 for garnish; chop remaining coarsely.
4. Sprinkle gelatin over water in a 1-cup measure. Let stand 5 minutes to soften; place cup in pan of simmering water until gelatin dissolves; remove from heat.
5. Combine egg yolks, ⅓ cup of the remaining sugar and the salt in a small bowl. Beat with electric mixer on high speed until very light, about 5 minutes.
6. Combine fruit mixture with gelatin; fold into yolk mixture along with chopped marrons. Chill until mixture is thick enough to mound.
7. Meanwhile, with clean beaters, beat egg whites until foamy-white in large bowl. Gradually beat in remaining sugar; continue beating until meringue forms soft peaks. Fold in yolk mixture and whipped cream. Spoon into prepared shell, piling high. (If mixture is too soft, chill briefly.)
8. Chill at least 4 hours. Decorate with additional whipped cream and reserved marrons. ● ● ●

Pictured opposite: (Clockwise from bottom) Sweet and Sour Pork with Noodles, page 456; Javanese Curried Noodles and Beef, page 456; Cantonese-Style Chow Mein, page 457

Neufchâtel

NEUFCHÂTEL A soft creamy cheese with a white crust originally made in Normandy, France. Neufchâtel is named after a town in that country-side. American Neufchâtel is similar to cream cheese except it has a lower butterfat content. It can be used in place of cream cheese. See also **CHEESE**.

NIÇOISE Foods prepared in the manner of Nice, France — with tomatoes, garlic, olive oil and ripe olives.

SALADE NIÇOISE

Makes 8 servings.

- 5 **medium-size potatoes, cooked, drained and cooled**
- 1 **pound green beans, cooked, drained and cooled**
- ⅔ **cup olive or vegetable oil**
- ⅓ **cup wine vinegar**
- 2 **cloves garlic, crushed**
- 1 **tablespoon Dijon mustard**
- 1 **tablespoon chopped fresh parsley**
- 1 **teaspoon salt**
- ¼ **teaspoon freshly ground pepper**
  Salad greens
- 2 **large tomatoes, cut into wedges**
- 1 **red onion, sliced**
- 1 **large green pepper, halved, seeded and cut into strips**
- 4 **hard-cooked eggs, sliced**
- 16 **pitted ripe olives**
- 1 **can (13 ounces) tuna, drained and broken into chunks**
- 1 **can (2 ounces) rolled anchovy fillets, drained**

1. Peel potatoes and cut into slices. Place in a shallow dish. Place beans in a second shallow dish.

2. Combine oil, vinegar, garlic, mustard, parsley, salt and pepper in a jar with a tight-fitting lid; shake well to mix. Drizzle ½ cup over the potatoes and 2 tablespoonfuls over the beans; let each stand at least 30 minutes to season.

3. Line a large salad bowl with salad greens. Arrange potatoes, green beans, tomatoes, onion, green pepper, eggs, olives, tuna and anchovies over greens. Drizzle with remaining dressing.

●●●

NOODLES A noodle is a flat-shaped pasta made of flour, water and eggs or egg solids. The other pasta products—macaroni and spaghetti—do not contain eggs and differ in their shapes.

Noodles will vary in width, length and shape. In the United States, by law, noodles must contain egg solids. Most Oriental noodles do not contain eggs and many are made of flour other than wheat. These Oriental noodles must be called "imitation noodles" or "alimentary paste noodles." Most noodles are made from semolina, which is milled from durum wheat. Other noodles may be made from rice, yam or mung beans.

American-made noodles are available in fine, medium or wide widths. Some may be shaped like bow ties; others may have vegetables such as spinach, carrots or tomatoes added for color and flavor. Noodles are an inexpensive standby for quick and delicious meals.

SWEET AND SOUR PORK WITH NOODLES

Makes 4 servings.

- 3 **quarts water**
- 1½ **pounds lean loin pork chops**
- 1 **egg, beaten**
- ¼ **cup all-purpose flour**
- 2 **tablespoons water**
- 1½ **teaspoons salt**
- 1 **can (8 ounces) pineapple chunks in pineapple juice**
- 1 **tablespoon cornstarch**
- 3 **tablespoons distilled white vinegar**
- 1 **tablespoon sugar**
- 2 **tablespoons soy sauce**
- ¼ **cup dry sherry**
- ¼ **cup vegetable oil**
- 1 **package (8 ounces) small curly noodles**
- 2 **green peppers, halved, seeded and cut into strips**
- ½ **cup chopped green onions**
- 2 **tomatoes, cut in wedges**

1. Heat water to boiling in a large covered kettle.

2. While water heats, remove pork meat from bones; cut into ½-inch pieces.

3. Combine egg, flour, water and ½ teaspoon salt in small bowl. Stir in pork to coat well.

4. Drain pineapple juice into a small bowl; add cornstarch, vinegar, sugar, soy sauce and sherry. Reserve.

5. Add ½ teaspoon of the oil and remaining 1 teaspoon of the salt to boiling water. Add noodles slowly so that water continues to boil. Cook about 5 minutes or until noodles are tender. Drain; keep warm.

6. Heat remaining oil in wok or skillet. Stir-fry pork until brown, about 5 minutes. Stir in green pepper, onions and reserved sauce from step 4; cover; cook 5 minutes longer.

7. Stir in pineapple chunks and tomato wedges. Serve hot over noodles.

JAVANESE CURRIED NOODLES AND BEEF

Makes 4 servings.

- 3 **quarts water**
- ¼ **teaspoon salt**
- 3½ **teaspoons vegetable oil**
- 2½ **cups curly broad noodles**
- ½ **cup catsup**
- 2 **tablespoons soy sauce**
- ¼ **teaspoon pepper**
- ¼ **cup water**
- 2 **to 3 teaspoons curry powder**
- ½ **cup chopped green onions**
- 1 **pound ground chuck**
- 1 **cup fresh bean sprouts**
  OR: 2 cups finely shredded romaine lettuce

1. Heat water to boiling in large covered kettle; add salt and ½ teaspoon of the oil. Add noodles slowly so that water continues to boil. Boil about 5 minutes until noodles are still slightly firm. Drain; place in large bowl; toss with 1 teaspoon of the oil. Keep warm.

2. Combine catsup, soy sauce, pepper and water in small bowl. Reserve.

3. Place wok or skillet over low heat; add curry; heat until fragrant, about 1 minute. Add remaining 2 teaspoons oil. Increase heat; add onions; stir-fry 1 minute. Add meat; stir-fry until no pink remains.

4. Stir in reserved catsup mixture; heat to boiling. Add noodles and bean sprouts. Stir and mix until hot. Garnish with green onion ruffles, if you wish.

CANTONESE-STYLE CHOW MEIN
Makes 6 servings.

- 1 package (10 ounces) frozen mixed Chinese-style vegetables in seasoned sauce
- 2 teaspoons cornstarch
- 1 tablespoon soy sauce
- 2 whole chicken breasts, skinned, boned and cut into thin strips
  OR: 2 cups slivered cooked chicken
- 3 to 4 teaspoons vegetable oil
- ¼ cup chopped green onions
- 1 can condensed chicken broth
- 2 tablespoons dry sherry
- 1½ cups very fine noodles (from an 8-ounce package)
- 1 package (8 ounces) frozen, cooked, shelled and deveined shrimp
- 2 cups finely shredded romaine lettuce
  OR: 1 cup fresh bean sprouts

1. Remove vegetables from package; let thaw in large bowl until vegetables can be separated with a fork.
2. Combine cornstarch and soy sauce with chicken in a medium-size bowl.
3. Heat a wok or large skillet until very hot. Add 3 teaspoons of the oil and chicken mixture. Stir-fry until chicken turns white and the pieces separate. (If using cooked chicken, stir-fry 30 seconds until hot.) Remove chicken to a plate with slotted spoon.
4. Add 1 more teaspoon of oil, if necessary; stir in green onions. Add broth and sherry; cover; bring to boiling; stir in noodles; let boil about 1 minute.
5. Stir in partially thawed vegetables; cook, uncovered, 1 minute. Add frozen shrimp and reserved chicken. Stir-fry until noodles are tender and chicken and shrimp are heated through.
6. Stir in lettuce; serve immediately.

FETTUCCINE WITH ASPARAGUS
Makes 4 servings.

- 1 package (12 ounces) fettuccine noodles
- 1½ pounds fresh asparagus, trimmed and cut into 1-inch lengths
- ¼ cup (½ stick) butter or margarine
- 1 medium-size onion, diced
- 1 cup chicken broth
- 4 eggs
- 1 teaspoon salt
- ¼ teaspoon pepper
- 1 cup freshly grated Parmesan cheese

1. Cook pasta in boiling salted water, following label directions, for a total of 9 minutes. Add asparagus to kettle during the last 5 minutes.
2. Meanwhile, melt butter in a small saucepan over moderate heat. Sauté onion in butter until soft. Stir in chicken broth and simmer 2 minutes.
3. Drain fettuccine and asparagus and return to kettle. Add onion mixture and toss. Remove from heat; add eggs, salt and pepper and toss quickly. Add cheese and toss again. Serve immediately with more cheese.

HOMEMADE EGG NOODLES
Makes about 1 pound uncooked noodles.

- 4 eggs
- 1 teaspoon salt
- 2¾ cups *sifted* all-purpose flour

1. Beat eggs well with salt in a medium-size bowl. Stir in 1 cup of the flour, then mix in enough of the remaining flour to form a stiff dough.
2. Turn out onto a lightly floured pastry cloth or board. Knead, adding a little extra flour to keep dough from sticking, 5 minutes or until smooth. Shape into a ball; cover with a bowl turned upside down. Let stand on board about 30 minutes. Divide in half.
3. Roll out, half at a time, into a large thin sheet; hang dough on a towel spread over the back of a straight-back chair. (Another idea is to make a rack by placing a long dowel or broom handle over the back of two chairs.) Let dough hang about 30 minutes or until dry but still workable.
4. Roll up each sheet, jelly-roll fashion; cut into ¼-inch-wide slices. Separate slices, then unroll strips; spread out on board. Let stand to dry, turning several times, about 30 minutes. Cut strips in half, if you wish. Cook, following your favorite recipe.

NOODLES ROMANOFF
Bake at 350° for 30 minutes.
Makes 6 servings.

- 1 package (8 ounces) medium-size noodles
- 1 container (8 ounces) creamed cottage cheese
- 1 container (8 ounces) dairy sour cream
- ½ cup grated Parmesan cheese
- 1 teaspoon grated onion
- 1 teaspoon Worcestershire sauce

1. Cook noodles in boiling salted water in a kettle, following label directions; drain; return to kettle.
2. Stir in the cottage cheese, sour cream, Parmesan cheese, onion and Worcestershire sauce; spoon into a 6-cup baking dish.
3. Bake in a moderate oven (350°) for 30 minutes or until hot.

FETTUCCINE VERDE
Makes 4 servings.

- 1 package (8 ounces) green or spinach noodles
- ½ cup (1 stick) butter or margarine
- 1 can (3 or 4 ounces) sliced mushrooms, drained
- 1 whole canned pimiento, drained and chopped
- ½ cup freshly grated Parmesan cheese
  Freshly ground pepper

1. Cook noodles following label directions. Drain and place on a large, heated, serving platter.
2. While noodles cook, melt butter in small saucepan; add mushrooms and pimiento; cook and stir until piping hot.
3. Pour butter mixture over noodles; add grated cheese and pepper; toss lightly until noodles are coated.

●●●

Nutmeg

NUTMEG The dry fruit or seed of the nutmeg tree, an evergreen native to the Spice Islands but now grown in the West Indies. The ripe fruit of a nutmeg tree resembles an apricot in size and color. When the fruit is harvested, the outer husk is stripped and discarded. The stripping is done carefully so that the membrane or skin covering the seed or nut is not destroyed. The skin is removed and sold as mace, another spice. (See also **MACE.**) The nut (or kernel) is dried and cracked. The kernel is known as whole nutmeg. Nutmeg is sold whole or ground. Use ground nutmeg for milk beverages, cakes and pastries.

NUTS Some of the dry fruits or seeds we call nuts are not considered nuts by botanists. For example, peanuts are legumes in the pea family; the almond belongs to the peach family; the cashew is really a part of the fruit of the cashew apple.

The outside covering of a nut is the rind or shell. The inner edible fruit is often called meat but is more accurately called a kernel.

Nuts are sold in the shell or shelled. Nuts in the shell are lower in cost per edible portion than shelled nuts and can be stored longer than shelled nuts. Look for nuts with clean, bright shells, not dirty or cracked. If buying nuts by weight, select nuts heavy for their size. A heavy nut is likely to contain a good, meaty kernel. Nuts should be stored in a cool, dry place to preserve freshness. They should not be shelled until ready to use.

Shelled nuts are sold in packages, jars or cans. They may be unroasted or roasted and salted. For the longest storage, keep shelled, unroasted nuts refrigerated or frozen. They should not be stored near strong-smelling foods because the kernels will absorb strong odors. If nuts are frozen, thaw and allow any moisture to evaporate before using.

See also specific nut.

Nut Preparation Tips

● *How to Blanch:* Almonds and peanuts both have, in addition to their shells, tightly clinging brown or reddish skins. For most recipes, the nuts must be blanched (skinned). The best way is to immerse the nuts in boiling water, dropping them into the water gradually so that the boiling doesn't stop, then to let them boil for about a minute. Drain the nuts, then slip off the skins with your fingers.

● *How to Chop Nuts:* The most efficient way is with a heavy French chopping knife. Place a small mound of nuts on a chopping block or board, then chop back and forth in an arc until they're the desired degree of fineness. Blenders can be used for chopping but they work so fast that they may overchop the nuts.

● *How to Grate Nuts:* If the nuts are to be grated very fine, use an electric blender or food processor. Do only about a cup of nuts at a time, stopping and stirring up from the bottom as needed to keep nuts from clumping. For more coarsely grated nuts, use a hand-held rotary grater.

SPICED NUTS

Bake at 300° for 10 minutes.
Makes 3 cups.

- ¼ **cup vegetable oil**
- 2 **teaspoons chili powder**
- ½ **teaspoon ground cumin**
- ½ **teaspoon ground turmeric**
  Pinch cayenne
- 3 **cups walnuts or pecans**
- ½ **teaspoon salt**

1. Combine oil, chili powder, cumin, turmeric and cayenne in a large skillet. Heat over low heat until oil is quite hot (do not let oil smoke). Remove from heat.
2. Add nuts to oil; stir until coated. Spread nuts in a paper toweling-lined shallow baking pan.
3. Bake in a slow oven (300°) for 10 minutes or until crisp. Sprinkle with salt. Cool and store in a covered container; keep up to 1 month.

NUT AND RAISIN BREAD

Bake at 375° for 50 minutes.
Makes 1 loaf.

- 2 **envelopes active dry yeast**
- ⅓ **cup nonfat dry milk powder**
- 2 **tablespoons honey**
- 2 **tablespoons molasses**
- 1 **teaspoon salt**
- ¼ **cup vegetable oil**
- 2 **cups very warm milk**
- 1½ **cups whole wheat flour**
- 1½ **cups all-purpose flour**
- ½ **cup raisins**
- ½ **cup walnuts, chopped**

1. Combine yeast, dry milk, honey, molasses, salt and oil in a large bowl. Stir in the very warm milk. ("Very warm," about 120° to 130°, should feel very warm to the hand.) Beat mixture until well blended, about 30 seconds.
2. Blend the whole wheat and all-purpose flours in a medium-size bowl. Stir 1½ cups of the flour mixture into the yeast mixture. Beat with electric mixer at medium speed for 2 minutes. Stir in another ½ cup of flour; beat 1 minute. Beat in raisins, walnuts and remaining flour by hand until a heavy, sticky dough forms. If dough seems too stiff, beat in 2 extra tablespoons of vegetable oil while adding the last of the flour.
3. Preheat oven to 375°. Turn dough into a well greased 9 × 5 × 3-inch loaf pan. Cover with a clean cloth and let rise in a warm place, away from drafts, about 20 minutes.
4. Bake in a preheated moderate oven (375°) for 50 minutes or until loaf sounds hollow when tapped with fingers. Remove from pan; cool.

SUGAR-CRUSTED NUTS

Makes 6 cups.

- 6 **cups unsalted mixed nuts**
- 2 **cups sugar**
- 1 **cup water**
- ½ **teaspoon ground nutmeg**

Combine ingredients in a large skillet. Bring mixture to boiling and boil hard, stirring constantly, until it reaches 238° on candy thermometer or until syrup coats nuts and turns amber. Pour nuts out onto a large, greased cookie sheet; separate with 2 forks into a thin layer; let cool until syrup hardens. Break into pieces; place in an airtight container and store in a cool, dry place.

● ● ●

OATS The grains of a grass-like plant in the cereal family. A grain of oats is covered with a husk that is removed, although there are some varieties of oats that are hulless. Oats are used to make rolled oats and oatmeal which are eaten as breakfast foods. Oats are used as animal feed also.

To make rolled oats, the grains are cleaned, sorted, dried to loosen the hulls and develop flavor, and then hulled and sterilized. The hulled, sterilized grains are then flattened into flakes. To make oatmeal, the hulled grains are cut into coarse to fine textures. The word oatmeal should be used for the ground meal of the grain but it is commonly used to describe the cooked cereal.

Oats are available as rolled, also known as old-fashioned oats, quick-cooking and instant oatmeal. Scotch oatmeal is coarsely ground oats made by cutting the oat grains with stone rather than steel rollers. Many ready-to-eat cereals are made from oats.

Oats are one of the most nutritious grains. They contain some protein, fat and minerals. In European countries, oats are eaten as a meal in porridges, in baked goods such as bannocks and breads, and as a meat extender. Oats cannot be used alone in making breads because they contain no gluten; combine with all-purpose flour for baking.

DATE 'N' OAT BAR COOKIES
Bake at 375° for 30 minutes.
Makes 16 squares.

- **1 large orange**
- **1 cup chopped pitted dates**
- **½ cup water**
- **½ teaspoon ground cinnamon**
- **1 cup *sifted* unbleached all-purpose flour**
- **¼ cup sugar**
- **1 cup rolled oats**
- **½ cup (1 stick) unsalted butter, softened**

1. Grate a tablespoon of rind from orange; reserve. Squeeze ¼ cup of juice.
2. Mix dates, water and orange juice in a small saucepan. Cook, stirring until thickened. Remove from heat and stir in reserved rind and cinnamon. Cool.
3. Sift flour into a large bowl. Stir in sugar and oats. Cut in butter with pastry blender until coarse crumbs form.
4. Preheat oven to 375°. Pat half of crumb mixture firmly into buttered 8 × 8 × 2-inch baking pan. Spread cooled filling evenly over top; sprinkle remaining crumb mixture over filling. Sprinkle with additional sugar.
5. Bake in a preheated moderate oven (375°) for 30 minutes or until top is very lightly browned. Cool; cut into squares.

CHOCOLATE COCONUT CRISPS
Bake at 350° for 12 minutes.
Makes about 7 dozen cookies.

- **⅔ cup *sifted* unbleached all-purpose flour**
- **⅓ cup unsweetened cocoa powder**
- **½ teaspoon baking soda**
- **½ teaspoon salt**
- **¾ cup (1½ sticks) unsalted butter, softened**
- **1 cup firmly packed brown sugar**
- **1 egg**
- **¼ cup water**
- **3 cups rolled oats**
- **1 cup flaked coconut**

1. Sift flour, cocoa, baking soda and salt onto wax paper. Beat the butter, sugar and egg in large bowl with electric mixer until fluffy; stir in water; blend well.
2. Stir flour mixture into butter mixture, blending well. Stir in oats and coconut.
3. Preheat oven to 350°. Drop by teaspoonfuls onto lightly greased cookie sheet. Dip fingertips in cold water; flatten cookies slightly.
4. Bake in a preheated moderate oven (350°) for 12 minutes. Cool on wire racks.

Oats

OATMEAL RAISIN COOKIES

Bake at 350° for 15 minutes.
Makes about 2½ dozen cookies.

- ½ cup (1 stick) unsalted butter, softened
- ½ cup firmly packed light brown sugar
- ¼ cup milk
- 1¼ cups *sifted* unbleached all-purpose flour
- 1¼ teaspoons ground cinnamon
- 1 cup rolled oats
- ⅓ cup raisins
- ⅓ cup chopped walnuts or pecans

1. Beat butter and sugar until fluffy in a bowl with electric mixer; stir in milk.
2. Sift flour and cinnamon onto wax paper. Stir in oats. Stir mixture into butter mixture until blended. Add raisins and nuts; mix well.
3. Preheat oven to 350°. Drop cookies by level tablespoonfuls on ungreased cookie sheets, about 2 inches apart. Dip fingertips in cold water; flatten cookies slightly.
4. Bake in a preheated moderate oven (350°) for 15 minutes or until lightly browned. Cool on wire racks.

OATMEAL BANNOCKS

Makes 8 bannocks.

- 1 cup lightly spooned all-purpose flour
- 1 teaspoon baking soda
- 1 teaspoon cream of tartar
- ½ teaspoon salt
- 1 cup quick oats
- 2 eggs
- 1 tablespoon honey
- 1½ cups milk

1. Sift the flour, baking soda and cream of tartar into a medium-size bowl. Stir in the salt and oats.
2. Beat the eggs, honey and milk in a small bowl until well mixed. Make a well in the center of the dry ingredients and add the liquids. Beat until smooth. Grease a griddle lightly; heat over low to medium heat. When griddle is hot, drop batter by spoonfuls without crowding. When bubbles form, turn and cook the other side for 2 to 3 minutes. Serve warm with butter and honey.

OATMEAL À LA MODE

Kids will love this for breakfast.
Makes 2 servings.

- ¼ cup shredded or flaked coconut
- ¼ cup slivered or sliced almonds
- 1½ cups water
- ¼ teaspoon ground cinnamon
- ⅔ cup quick oats
- ⅓ cup raisins
- 1 pint vanilla ice cream

1. Heat coconut and almonds in medium-size saucepan until golden brown, stirring frequently for even browning. Remove and place on paper toweling.
2. Bring water and cinnamon to boiling in same saucepan. Stir in oats and raisins. Bring to boiling. Cover and simmer over low heat 1 minute.
3. Remove from heat. Let stand 1 minute. Spoon into 2 bowls. Serve with scoop of ice cream on top of each; sprinkle with coconut and almonds.

OIL A fluid substance extracted or pressed from vegetables, fruits or seeds. Cooking or salad oils are primarily obtained from vegetables or seeds. Essential oils, which are used as flavoring substances, are obtained from fruits and some herbs.

Vegetable oils, also often called salad oil and sometimes cooking oil, can be made from corn, cottonseeds, olives, peanuts, sesame seeds, safflowers or soy beans. Most are light amber in color and have no odor or flavor. The exceptions are olive, peanut and sesame oils, each of which has a distinct flavor. Olive oil is the choice for salads; peanut and sesame oils are preferred for Oriental dishes. Store oil in a cool, dry place. Oil can become rancid if moisture is present in it.

OKRA The immature seed pod of a hibiscus plant, used principally in soups and stews. Okra makes a tasty vegetable appetizer when dipped into beaten egg thinned with a tablespoon water and then rolled in seasoned cracker crumbs or cornmeal and deep-fried in oil. Serve fried okra dipped in bottled chili sauce.

Okra was discovered in Ethiopia and cultivated in Egypt, then taken to Europe by the Moors. It was introduced to New Orleans by the French colonists and Africans. It is grown extensively in the South. Okra is called *gumbo* because it is used to thicken a soup-stew by that name. (See also **GUMBO.**) Okra is a natural thickener because of its mucilaginous consistency which develops during long cooking.

Buying and Storing: Okra is available fresh in some markets all year but the peak season is summer. Okra may be green or greenish-white in color with pods that are either long and thin or short and chunky. Select pods that are crisp and 2 to 4 inches long. Allow 1 pound for 3 to 4 servings. Refrigerate unwashed okra in a plastic bag in the vegetable crisper in the refrigerator; use within a week. Okra is also available frozen and canned. Another variety of okra found in Oriental markets is called Chinese okra or luffa. It looks like the African okra but grows up to a foot long, feels spongy and tastes like cooked cucumber. It is pared before cooking quickly.

To Prepare and Cook: Wash and trim stem ends. (Only the Chinese variety is pared.) Okra can be sliced or if small, left whole. Okra is always eaten cooked. Proper cooking of African okra will overcome the pastiness. Also, pastiness can be avoided if the pods are left whole or cooked briefly. Okra can be boiled, baked or fried. It combines well with corn and tomatoes. To cook cut-up okra, drop into a saucepan with an inch of boiling water; cover and cook 5 minutes. Drain and season with butter and lemon juice or tomato sauce.

OKRA WITH FISH

Makes 6 servings.

- 1½ pounds fresh okra, trimmed and finely diced
- 1½ pounds fresh (or frozen) whiting, boned and cut into thin strips
- 1 medium onion, diced (½ cup)

½ teaspoon salt
¼ teaspoon pepper

Combine all ingredients in a large saucepan. Add enough cold water to barely cover mixture. Bring to boiling; lower heat. Cook, uncovered, for 3 to 5 minutes. Okra should be slightly crunchy and green.

— • • • —

OLIVES For at least 4,000 years, olives have been a dietary staple in the Mediterranean countries. The gnarled evergreen olive tree with its small leaves was first cultivated in the ideal climate of the Middle East. It was brought to California in the 1700's by Franciscan monks.

No one is certain how man discovered that the bitter fruit of the olive tree could be eaten. All olives are equally forbidding when freshly picked because of a natural substance called glucoside. Credit for the discovery is given to shepherds who observed their flocks nibbling on the fruit of an olive branch that had fallen into a stream. It was this leaching in water that removed the acrid substance. The leaching done today is by means of a salt and water brine or salt alone.

Once rid of bitterness, olives can take on their own flavor qualities, depending upon final processing. They are harvested at various degrees of ripeness according to the style of olive cure and place of origin.

Spanish-style cured olives are picked when immature or green. When olives are tree ripened, they become black and very soft. Consequently, they cannot withstand processing as whole fruit but are the proper stage to be pressed to extract the oil. Ripe olives, produced in California, are picked when partially ripe, just as they are turning from green to golden brown. During processing, if ripe olives are protected from air, they do not darken and are canned as green ripe olives. If air is bubbled into the brine, the olives oxidize and turn the familiar black color.

Most of the olives on supermarket shelves are either ripe olives or Spanish-style cured olives. In some markets, you will find olives originating from Greece, Italy, France, Morocco, South America and even China.

Here is a brief description of the olives available.

Ripe olives: Two types of ripe olives are sold—green and black. Green ripe olives are mild-tasting and mottled with specks of brown; usually sold unpitted. Black ripe olives come in numerous sizes from small to jumbo. Size grades are determined by the number of olives per pound. Black ripe olives are whole, unpitted or pitted, halved, wedged, sliced or chopped. Ripe olives are grown and processed in California, and canned in salted water.

Spanish-style or Spanish olives: These green olives are crisp and acidic. Most are pitted and stuffed with pimientos; always sold in jars, never in cans. Spanish olives are leached with a caustic lye solution rather than saltwater. The lye keeps the flesh crisp. After many rinses to remove the lye, the olives are covered with a salt and sugar brine and allowed to ferment for a month in a warm place. The salt and heat interact to produce lactic acid, giving these olives a pickled taste. After fermentation, the olives are ready for grading, pitting and stuffing. Olives can also be stuffed with tiny onions, almonds or anchovies. Spanish olives can be hand-packed in jars so that the olives are in perfect order, or machine-packed, which gives the olives a tousled appearance and causes the stuffing to separate. Use the more expensive hand-packed olives when appearance is important. Machine-packed olives, sometimes called salad olives, are ideal for recipes calling for chopped or diced Spanish olives. This style of olive originated in Spain.

Calamata olives: Shiny, almond-shaped, purple-black olives from Greece. They are traditionally slit and cured in olive oil, vinegar and salt. Some are cured in brine alone, drained, then packed in jars with oil and vinegar.

Greek olives: These are round, meaty, pungent, brine-cured black olives; also cured in California.

Sicilian olives: These small, oval green olives are cured in salt brine. Vinegar and spices such as hot red pepper, fennel and garlic are added, giving them a spicy, pickled flavor.

Nicoise olives: These tiny, black olives, primarily used to make olive oil, are cured in brine and packed with oil and sometimes herbs.

Moroccan olives: These small, black, wrinkled olives are partially sun-dried and cured with dry salt, then rubbed with olive oil. They have a mildly bitter taste. This style of olives is cured in California.

Alfonso olives: Large, purple South American olives brine-cured and packed in jars with oil and vinegar.

Dried olives: Tree-ripened, unpitted, cured olives, salted and sun-dried. The taste is piquant and salty. They are produced in Italy and China.

Fresh olives: Green olives, freshly picked, are available in some markets in September. With some effort, you can process or cure them at home.

TOMATO SALAD PASTA

Makes 4 servings.

1 package (16 ounces) rigatoni
1 small clove garlic, minced
½ teaspoon salt
2 tablespoons red wine vinegar
6 tablespoons olive oil
¼ teaspoon pepper
1 tablespoon leaf basil, crumbled
4 cups diced ripe tomatoes
⅓ cup diced red onion
½ cup small pitted ripe olives
1 package (8 ounces) whole milk mozzarella cheese, finely diced
½ cup grated Parmesan cheese

1. Cook pasta following label directions.
2. Mash garlic with salt in a medium-size bowl. Stir in vinegar, oil, pepper and basil. Add the tomatoes, onion and olives and toss to mix.
3. Drain pasta and return to kettle. Add cheeses and toss until heat of pasta begins to melt cheese. Add tomato mixture and toss again.

MIXED SALAD WITH OLIVES

Makes 4 servings.

- 1 jar (6 ounces) marinated artichoke hearts
- 1 jar (4 ounces) pimientos, drained
- 1 can (6 ounces) pitted ripe olives
- 1 medium-size head escarole or romaine
- 2 tablespoons sliced green onion
- 2 tablespoons lemon juice
- ½ teaspoon salt
- ¼ teaspoon pepper

1. Remove artichokes from jar with fork, reserving marinade. Halve the hearts lengthwise, if large, and place in bottom of salad bowl.
2. Pat pimientos dry between paper toweling; cut into slivers and place in bowl. Drain olives and place in bowl.
3. Tear lettuce into bite-size pieces; place in bowl; cover with plastic wrap.
4. Add green onion, lemon juice, salt and pepper to marinade in jar; cover. Refrigerate with salad. Shake dressing and toss with salad when ready to serve.

CHICKEN TIJUANA

Bake at 350° for 50 minutes.
Makes 4 servings.

- 1 broiler-fryer (about 2½ pounds)
- 2 cups water
- ¼ teaspoon salt
- ½ cup all-purpose flour
- 2 tablespoons butter or margarine
- 3 tablespoons vegetable oil
- 3 medium-size tomatoes, peeled and quartered
- ¼ cup pimiento-stuffed olives, sliced
- 1 large onion, chopped (1 cup)
- 1 large green pepper, halved, seeded and chopped
- 1 teaspoon leaf basil, crumbled
- 1 teaspoon seasoned salt
- 1 teaspoon paprika
- ⅓ cup grated Parmesan cheese

1. Cut wings from chicken. Remove giblets and neck from chicken package and place (except liver) with wings, water and the ¼ teaspoon salt

in a small saucepan; cover. Simmer 45 minutes. Add liver; cover; cook 15 minutes longer. Strain broth into a small bowl; reserve for Step 4. Chop giblets and the meat from wings and neck; reserve.
2. Cut chicken into serving-size pieces. Shake chicken, a few pieces at a time, in a plastic bag with flour to coat; tap off excess. Reserve 1 tablespoon of the flour for Step 4.
3. Sauté chicken in butter and oil in a large skillet, turning once, about 15 minutes or until golden brown. Place chicken in a 10-cup baking dish. Add tomatoes and olives.
4. Add onion and green pepper to drippings in skillet; sauté until tender. Stir in basil, the 1 tablespoon reserved flour, seasoned salt and paprika. Cook 1 minute, stirring constantly. Stir in 1 cup of the reserved broth; cook and stir until sauce thickens and bubbles 1 minute. Stir in chopped chicken and giblets and cheese. Pour over chicken and vegetables; cover.
5. Bake in a moderate oven (350°) for 50 minutes or until chicken is tender.

— • ● ● —

OMELET (Also **omelette**) This popular dish is a combination of eggs beaten with water or milk and seasonings. It is cooked in a small skillet or omelet pan until firm and can be filled with cooked meat, cheese or vegetables. This type of omelet is called a French omelet. A puffy omelet is another type of omelet in which the eggs are separated and the egg whites beaten until stiff. The egg yolks are folded into the egg whites with seasonings and then cooked in a skillet. This type of omelet is light and fluffy.

FRENCH OMELET

Makes 1 serving.

- 2 eggs
- 2 tablespoons water
  Salt and pepper
- 1 tablespoon butter or margarine

1. Beat the eggs with water in a small bowl until blended; season with salt and pepper.
2. Heat a small, heavy skillet slowly until it is very hot. Add butter and

swirl pan to coat entire surface. *Do not allow butter to brown.*
3. Pour egg mixture into skillet. As soon as eggs begin to set, start lifting the edge of egg mixture all the way around with a spatula until all the liquid has cooked.
4. To turn omelet out, tip pan, lift edge with a spatula; fold omelet over onto plate.

Toppings for French Omelet: Add just before folding omelet.

1. Sprinkle with chopped fresh parsley, watercress or chives.
2. Spread lightly with jam, jelly or marmalade for a dessert omelet.
3. Top with thinly sliced Gruyère, Swiss or shredded Cheddar cheese.

POTATO ZUCCHINI OMELET

Bake at 375° for 20 minutes.
Makes 6 servings.

- 8 eggs
- 2 tablespoons milk
- ¾ teaspoon salt
- ⅛ teaspoon pepper
- 4 tablespoons vegetable oil
- 1 small onion, chopped (¼ cup)
- 2 large all-purpose potatoes (about ¾ pound), pared and grated
- 2 zucchini, thinly sliced
- 1 tablespoon butter or margarine
- ½ cup grated Parmesan cheese
- 1 large tomato, sliced
  Watercress

1. Preheat oven to 375°. Beat eggs, milk, salt and pepper in a bowl.
2. Heat 3 tablespoons of the oil in a large skillet with ovenproof handle. Add onion and potatoes and cook, stirring constantly, until potatoes are almost tender, about 3 minutes. Stir into egg mixture. Wipe skillet clean.
3. Add remaining 1 tablespoon oil to skillet and sauté zucchini until tender. Remove to paper toweling.
4. Melt butter in skillet. Add egg-potato mixture; top with half of the cheese, zucchini and then the remaining cheese.
5. Bake in a preheated moderate oven (375°) for 20 minutes or until a knife inserted in the center of the omelet comes out clean. Loosen around edges with metal spatula.

ROLLED SHRIMP AND SPROUT OMELET

This rolled, puffy omelet is really a soufflé mixture baked in a pan instead of a soufflé dish.

Bake at 400° for 25 to 30 minutes.
Makes one 10-inch roll or 6 servings.

Roll:
- ¼ cup (½ stick) butter or margarine
- ½ cup all-purpose flour
- 1 teaspoon salt
- 2 cups milk
- 6 eggs, separated

Filling:
- 1 tablespoon vegetable oil
- ½ pound shrimp, shelled, deveined and diced (1 cup)
- ½ pound bean sprouts, coarsely chopped (3½ cups)
- 1 bunch green onions, thinly sliced, both green and white parts (1½ cups)
- 1 tablespoon cornstarch
- 1 tablespoon dry sherry
- 1 teaspoon salt
  Dash cayenne
- 1 package (3 ounces) cream cheese, cubed

1. Prepare Roll: Melt butter in a medium-size saucepan. Stir in flour and salt; cook 1 minute. Remove from heat; stir in milk gradually. Cook, stirring constantly, until mixture is thick.
2. Beat egg yolks in a medium-size bowl. Slowly beat one half of hot mixture into yolks until blended. Stir yolk mixture into remaining hot mixture. Cook and stir 1 minute more. Remove from heat. Cover surface of sauce with plastic wrap to prevent skin from forming. Refrigerate until cool.
3. Preheat oven to 400°. Butter a 15½ × 10½ × 1-inch jelly-roll pan; line bottom with wax paper; butter paper; dust with flour.
4. Beat egg whites in a large bowl until soft peaks form. Fold in cooled sauce mixture until no streaks of yellow remain. Spread evenly in pan.
5. Bake in a preheated hot oven (400°) for 25 minutes or until firm and browned.
6. While roll bakes, prepare Filling: Heat oil in large skillet; add shrimp; sauté 1 minute just until shrimp turn pink. Stir in bean sprouts and onions. Cook until onions are just wilted. Combine cornstarch, sherry, salt and cayenne in small cup. Add to skillet; cook, stirring constantly, until thickened. Stir in cream cheese until blended. Cool slightly.
7. Remove roll from oven. Loosen around edges with spatula; cover with clean towel or foil. Place a large cookie sheet on top; then quickly turn jelly-roll pan upside down. Lift pan; peel off paper.
8. Spread filling over surface of roll. Starting at short end, roll up jelly-roll fashion, lifting away towel or foil. Lift roll onto cutting board with two wide spatulas. Cut into slices to serve.

PUFFY SPANISH OMELET

Bake at 350° for 10 minutes.
Makes 4 servings.

- 6 eggs, separated
- 6 tablespoons milk or water
- 1 teaspoon salt
- ¼ teaspoon pepper
- 4 tablespoons (½ stick) butter or margarine
- 1 medium-size onion, sliced
- 1 small green pepper, seeded and diced (½ cup)
- ¼ teaspoon leaf marjoram, crumbled
- ⅛ teaspoon cayenne
- 3 medium-size tomatoes, peeled and coarsely chopped
- 1 cup dairy sour cream
- 2 tablespoons snipped chives

1. Beat egg whites until stiff in a large bowl with electric mixer.
2. Beat egg yolks slightly in a medium-size bowl with same mixer. Add milk, ½ teaspoon of the salt and pepper, beating until thick. Fold into egg white mixture thoroughly.
3. Preheat oven to 350°. Heat a 10-inch skillet or omelet pan with an ovenproof handle. Swirl 2 tablespoons of the butter over bottom and side of skillet.
4. Pour in egg mixture. Cook over low heat 5 minutes or until mixture is set on the bottom and is golden brown.
5. Bake in a preheated moderate oven (350°) for 10 minutes or until puffy and golden on the top.
6. While omelet is baking, sauté onion and green pepper in remaining 2 tablespoons butter in a large skillet until soft, about 5 minutes. Add marjoram, remaining salt, cayenne and tomatoes; cook just until hot.
7. Remove omelet from oven. Loosen around edge with a knife; cut a gash with knife down center of omelet; place tomato mixture down one side of omelet; fold over with pancake turner; turn onto heated serving platter. Top with sour cream and chives. Serve at once.

CORN OMELET

Bake at 325° for 2 minutes.
Makes 4 servings.

- 2 large ears of corn
- 6 bacon slices
- 4 tablespoons (½ stick) butter or margarine
- 1 large onion, thinly sliced
- 1 cup diced green pepper
- 6 eggs
- 1 teaspoon salt
- ¼ teaspoon pepper
  Few drops liquid hot pepper seasoning

1. Scrape corn from cobs (you should have 1 cup). Cook corn in boiling unsalted water to cover in a small saucepan 3 to 5 minutes or until tender; drain; spoon into a large bowl. Preheat oven to 325°.
2. Cook bacon in a large skillet until crisp and brown. Drain on paper toweling; crumble; add to corn. Pour bacon drippings into a cup. Measure and return 1 tablespoon to skillet. Add 2 tablespoons of the butter and heat until melted. Sauté onion and pepper until tender; add to corn.
3. Add eggs, salt, pepper and liquid hot pepper seasoning to bowl with corn mixture; beat until mixed.
4. Wipe the skillet out with paper toweling. Heat the remaining 2 tablespoons butter with 1 tablespoon of the bacon drippings until very hot. Add the egg mixture and cook until bottom is set, but top is still liquid.
5. Bake in a preheated slow oven (325°) for 2 minutes or until top is set

NORMANDY OMELET

For a breakfast or supper treat try this puffy omelet with its apple filling.

Bake at 350° for 8 to 10 minutes.
Makes 4 servings as a dessert, or 2 servings as breakfast.

- **4 tablespoons (½ stick) butter or margarine**
- **2 tablespoons honey**
- **¼ teaspoon ground cinnamon**
- **1 can (20 ounces) unsweetened apple slices**
- **½ teaspoon grated lemon rind**
- **4 eggs, separated**
- **2 tablespoons sugar**
- **¼ cup heavy cream**
- **10X (confectioners') sugar**

1. Heat 2 tablespoons of the butter in small skillet; stir in honey and cinnamon; heat until bubbly. Add apples and lemon rind; heat through; keep warm.

2. Beat egg whites with 1 tablespoon of the sugar in a large bowl with rotary beater until stiff peaks form. Using same beaters, beat egg yolks with remaining sugar until light and thick; then beat in cream, 1 tablespoon at a time. Fold egg yolks into whites, using a rubber spatula, until thoroughly blended.

3. Preheat oven to 350°. Heat a 9- or 10-inch heavy ovenproof skillet over medium heat. Add remaining butter to skillet; tilt pan to cover side with butter. As the butter foams and then subsides (do not allow to brown), pour in egg mixture. Spread mixture evenly in pan; cook over low heat, without stirring, until omelet is golden brown on underside, about 5 minutes.

4. Bake in a preheated moderate oven (350°) for 8 to 10 minutes or until omelet feels firm when pressed with fingertip.

5. To serve: Ease half of omelet onto serving platter. Spoon apple filling over, then fold other half over filling or serve right from skillet. Sprinkle top with 10X sugar.

— ● ● ● —

ONION A vegetable used for centuries as a flavoring ingredient, the onion is a bulb-like plant in the *Allium* or lily family, related to tulips and hyacinths, garlic, leeks, chives and shallots.

Buying and Storing: There are many varieties of onions of varying sizes and colors. Onions are marketed either dry or fresh. Freshly harvested onions have leafy green tops and the bulb is covered with a soft, pliable skin. When onions are allowed to dry, the tops die and the skin turns dry and papery and cracks easily. Most onions are marketed in this way. The only fresh onions marketed are green onions and scallions. Onions are also sold in packages in a dehydrated form, such as instant minced onions.

Here is a listing of the varieties available.

Bermuda: These may have yellow or white skin and flat-shaped bulbs about 3 to 4 inches in diameter. The flesh is sweet, mild and juicy. Look for them from March through June and use for serving in salads, topping sandwiches, browning with steak or for deep-fat frying. These do not store well so buy only what you can use quickly.

Cocktail: Tiny, white onions sold in pint containers. They are also called *pearl* onions. These tiny onions are also frozen, or pickled and sold in jars.

Green: The terms green onion and scallion are used interchangeably. Technically they are different. Green onions are onions that are harvested green or before maturity and have a small bulb similar to dry onions. Green onions have leaves from 8 to 24 inches long and can be any variety of onion. Scallions are any shoots from white onion varieties that are pulled before the bulb forms. Both green onions and scallions are mild enough to serve raw as an appetizer, or sliced and added to salads or cottage cheese. They are also elegant when poached like asparagus and sauced with cheese. Green onions and scallions are sold in bunches year-round. Refrigerate; use within 3 days.

Red or Italian: Because of its deep maroon skin, this type is probably the most beautiful of all onions. Its mild, sweet flavor is ideal for salads and sandwiches. Available from March to December.

Scallions: Similar to green onions but with slim rather than bulbous ends. See **green onions** above.

Spanish: Nicknamed the "Gentle Giant," these onions are one of the largest—some measure as much as 5 inches in diameter. Originally introduced from Spain, these onions are globe-shaped with a pale yellow to tan skin. The flesh is firm and mild-tasting. The biggest supply comes from Idaho and Oregon, available from August through March. Store in a cool, dry place.

White: Available as small, boiling onions or larger sizes for general use. Small boiling onions, 1 to 1½ inches in diameter, are cooked whole in stew or can be glazed or creamed to serve as a vegetable. There are 18 to 24 small onions in a pound. The larger white onions range in size from 2 to 3 inches in diameter. They are available year-round.

Yellow: This type, sometimes called brown onions, is the old reliable of the onion family. Some are globe-shaped, others flat-shaped bulbs. The skin is tan; sizes range from small to large. Available year-round; store in a cool, dry place.

Onion Nutrition: Onions are low in calories and provide the diet with vitamin C. A 3½-ounce serving is about 38 calories.

Onion Math
1½ pounds small white onions = 4 servings
1 small onion = ¼ cup chopped
1 medium = ½ cup chopped
1 large onion = 1 cup chopped

Onion Preparation Tips

● To peel small white onions quickly, cover with boiling water; let stand several minutes; drain and cover with cold water. Remove skins.

● To dice or chop an onion, peel onion and cut in half from stem to root end. Place, cut-side down, on a board; slice onion about ¼-inch thick. Keeping slices together, rotate a quarter turn and slice again.

Pictured opposite: Puffy Spanish Omelet, page 463

Onion

ONION SOUP

Bake at 425° for 10 minutes, then broil quickly to brown.
Makes 6 servings.

- **4 large onions, sliced**
- **¼ cup (½ stick) butter or margarine**
- **6 cups beef broth**
  Salt and pepper
- **6 slices French bread, toasted**
- **½ cup grated Parmesan cheese**
- **1 ounce Gruyère or Swiss cheese, shredded (¼ cup)**

1. Sauté onions in butter in Dutch oven for 15 minutes or until lightly browned. Stir in beef broth. Bring to boiling; lower heat; cover; simmer 30 minutes. (Soup may be prepared ahead to this point. Reheat and add the bread and cheese just before serving.) Add salt and pepper to taste.
2. Preheat oven to 425°. Ladle soup into 6 ovenproof soup bowls or six 12-ounce custard cups or an 8-cup casserole. Lay bread slices on top; sprinkle with cheeses. Place bowls or cups in a jelly-roll pan or shallow baking pan.
3. Bake in a preheated hot oven (425°) for 10 minutes, then place under preheated broiler and broil until top is bubbly and lightly browned.

PICKLED ONIONS

Cheddar cheese, bread and beer are the perfect accompaniments for pickled onions.

Makes 2 cups.

- **1 pound small white onions**
  Boiling water
- **1 cup cold water**
- **2 tablespoons salt**
- **1⅔ cups malt vinegar**
- **⅓ cup cold water**
- **⅓ cup sugar**
- **1 tablespoon mixed pickling spices tied in cheesecloth bag**
- **¼ teaspoon maple flavoring**

1. Place onions in a large bowl; cover with boiling water; let stand 2 minutes; drain. Cover with cold water. Cut off root end and slip off skins; return onions to bowl.
2. Combine the 1 cup water with salt. Pour over onions; cover; let stand overnight. Drain; rinse thoroughly with cold water; drain again.
3. Combine vinegar, ⅓ cup water, sugar, spice bag and maple flavoring in a large saucepan; bring to boiling. Add onions and return to boiling; remove spice bag; cool. Spoon into a large jar or bowl; cover. Refrigerate overnight.

ONION-LEMON RELISH

Serve with meat or poultry.
Makes about 1½ cups.

- **2 large lemons**
- **6 green onions with green tops, cut up**
- **½ green pepper, seeded**
- **¼ cup parsley sprigs**
- **1 cup chopped celery**
- **½ teaspoon dry mustard**
- **¼ teaspoon ground cardamom**
- **1 teaspoon salt**
- **1 small hot red pepper, seeded and chopped**
  OR: ½ teaspoon liquid hot pepper seasoning
- **1 tablespoon sugar**

1. Grate lemons and reserve the grated rind. Cut off all the remaining white membrane of lemons.
2. Put lemons, green onions, pepper, parsley and celery through the coarse blade of a meat grinder, or whirl in a food processor until coarsely chopped. Stir in grated lemon rind.
3. Add mustard, cardamom, salt, chopped pepper and sugar. Refrigerate, covered, overnight to blend flavors.

ONION PIE

Bake at 375° for 35 minutes.
Makes one 10-inch pie.

- **6 large onions, sliced**
- **¼ cup (½ stick) butter or margarine**
- **2 tablespoons flour**
- **1 teaspoon salt**
- **¼ teaspoon pepper**
- **1½ cups milk**
- **1 package piecrust mix**
- **2 hard-cooked eggs, sliced**

1. Cook onion slices in boiling salted water to cover in a large saucepan 10 minutes or just until tender-firm; drain well.
2. While onions cook, melt butter in a medium-size saucepan. Blend in flour, salt and pepper; slowly stir in milk. Cook, stirring constantly, until sauce thickens slightly and bubbles 3 minutes. Remove from heat.
3. Preheat oven to 375°. Prepare piecrust mix following label directions. Roll out ⅔ to a 14-inch round on lightly floured surface; fit into 10-inch pie plate. Trim overhang to ½ inch.
4. Arrange onions on bottom crust; top with eggs; pour sauce over. Roll out remaining pastry to a 12-inch round; cut several slits near center. Place over filling; pinch edges to seal. Turn edge up and in to seal in juices.
5. Bake in a preheated moderate oven (375°) for 35 minutes or until pastry is golden and juices bubble up near center. Cool on wire rack. Serve warm.

ONION AND EGG BAKE

A creamy casserole for onion lovers.
Bake at 350° for 30 minutes.
Makes 6 servings.

- **2 large Spanish onions (2½ pounds)**
- **¼ cup (½ stick) butter or margarine**
- **1 can condensed cream of mushroom soup, undiluted**
- **½ cup milk**
- **1 teaspoon salt**
- **¼ to ½ teaspoon leaf tarragon, crumbled**
- **¼ teaspoon pepper**
- **8 hard-cooked eggs, sliced**
- **¼ cup grated Parmesan cheese**

1. Peel, quarter and thinly slice onions. (You will have about 8 cups.)
2. Melt butter in large skillet; add onions. Sauté, stirring often, until tender but not browned. Stir in soup, milk, salt, tarragon and pepper.
3. Cover the bottom of a 2-quart casserole with a thin layer of onion mixture. Add a layer of egg slices. Repeat layers until all ingredients are used, ending with onion mixture. Sprinkle with cheese.
4. Bake in a moderate oven (350°) for 30 minutes or until hot and bubbly.

Pictured opposite: Onion Soup, page 466

Onion

BAKED MEAT-STUFFED SPANISH ONIONS

Bake at 375° for 1 hour.
Makes 4 servings.

- 4 large Spanish onions (each about 4 inches in diameter), peeled
- 1 tablespoon butter or margarine
- 1 can (13¾ ounces) beef broth
- 1 package (8 ounces) herb-seasoned stuffing mix
- ¾ pound ground round
- ¼ cup grated Parmesan cheese
- ¼ teaspoon ground nutmeg
- 2 eggs
- ⅓ cup dry white wine

1. Cut off a thin slice from the top of each onion. Scoop out insides with a spoon or melon baller, leaving a ¼-inch thick shell. Chop enough of the onion to measure ½ cup. (Use remaining onion for another recipe.)
2. Sauté onion in butter in a medium-size saucepan until soft but not brown. Add ½ cup of the beef broth and bring to boiling. Remove from heat and stir in stuffing mix. Add beef, cheese, nutmeg and eggs; mix thoroughly. Spoon beef mixture evenly into onion shells, mounding high. Place onions in a shallow baking dish and add remaining 1¼ cups beef broth and wine; cover dish with foil.
3. Bake in a moderate oven (375°) for 1 hour, basting after 30 minutes. Serve onions with pan juices.

FRENCH-FRIED ONION RINGS

Makes 4 servings.

- 2 very large yellow or Bermuda onions
- 2 eggs
- ½ cup milk
- 1 cup *sifted* all-purpose flour
- 1 teaspoon baking powder
- ½ teaspoon salt
  Vegetable oil for frying

1. Peel onions; cut into ¼-inch thick slices; separate into rings.
2. Beat eggs and milk until frothy in a large bowl; sift in flour, baking powder and salt; stir with a wire whisk just until blended.
3. Pour enough oil into a large skillet to make a depth of 1 inch. Heat to 375°

on a deep-fat frying thermometer.
4. Dip onion rings, a few at a time, into batter; drop into heated oil. Fry, turning once or twice until crisp and golden. Drain on paper toweling. To keep them warm until all the onion rings have been fried, place them on paper toweling-lined jelly-roll pan in preheated very slow oven (200°). (If batter is too thick, add 1 or 2 tablespoons milk.) Sprinkle fried onion rings with salt, if you wish. Serve hot.

BUTTER-BRAISED ONIONS

Makes 8 servings.

- 40 small white onions
- 3 tablespoons butter or margarine
- 1 teaspoon sugar
  Salt and pepper

1. Peel onions; cut an "x" in the root end of each onion. Cook, covered, in boiling salted water in a large saucepan until tender, about 15 minutes. Drain.
2. Heat butter in same saucepan just until it starts to brown. Add onions and sprinkle with sugar. Cook, stirring often, until golden and slightly glazed. Season with salt and pepper to taste.

ONIONS MORNAY

Bake at 350° for 30 minutes.
Makes 6 servings.

- ¼ cup (½ stick) butter or margarine
- 2 Bermuda onions, chopped (4 cups)
- 2 cloves garlic, minced
- 1 can condensed cream of celery soup
- 1 cup milk
- ¼ teaspoon seasoned pepper
- 1 can (16 ounces) cut green beans, drained
- 2 packages (8 ounces each) sliced process Swiss cheese
- 12 half-inch thick slices French bread

1. Melt butter or margarine in a large skillet; stir in the onions and garlic; cover. Cook 15 minutes; stir in soup, milk and pepper; heat, stirring several times, until bubbly.

2. Make two layers each of beans, cheese slices and sauce in a buttered, 8-cup baking dish; arrange bread slices, overlapping, on top.
3. Bake in a moderate oven (350°) for 30 minutes or until bubbly hot.

CREAMED ONIONS

Makes 8 servings.

- 40 small white onions
- 6 tablespoons butter or margarine
- 6 tablespoons flour
- 1½ teaspoons salt
- ¼ teaspoon white pepper
- ¼ teaspoon ground nutmeg
- 3 cups milk
- ½ cup heavy cream

1. Peel onions; cut an "x" in the root end. Cook onions, covered, in boiling salted water in a large saucepan until tender, about 15 minutes. Drain.
2. Melt butter in same saucepan. Stir in flour, salt, pepper and nutmeg; cook 2 minutes. Remove pan from heat; gradually stir in milk and heavy cream until smooth.
3. Bring to boiling; lower heat; simmer about 5 minutes, stirring constantly, until sauce is thick and smooth. Stir in onions.

COOKED ONION SALAD

Makes 4 to 6 servings.

- 4 large yellow onions (about 1½ pounds)
- ⅓ cup bacon drippings
- ½ teaspoon salt
- ¼ teaspoon freshly ground pepper
- 1 tablespoon flour
- 3 tablespoons wine or cider vinegar (or to taste)
- 1 tablespoon chopped fresh parsley

1. Cut onions into ¼-inch thick slices. Sauté onions in drippings in a large skillet until soft. (Do not brown.) Drain off excess drippings.
2. Sprinkle salt, pepper and flour over onions; mix lightly with a fork. Add vinegar; cook, stirring constantly with a fork, 2 to 3 minutes. Transfer to serving dish; sprinkle with parsley.

●●●

ORANGE This popular citrus fruit probably originated in southern Asia or China. The Spaniards introduced oranges to Florida in the 16th century and to California in the 18th century. Oranges are classified into three types: sweet, sour and mandarin. There are numerous varieties within each type.

Sweet oranges are the most popular for general eating because the pulp is sweet and juicy. The best known varieties include navel, Valencia, Jaffa and blood oranges. Navel is a seedless orange, available in quantity from November to May. Valencia oranges are shipped from Florida, February to June, and from California from late April to October. Jaffa and blood oranges are in season from mid-March to May. Blood oranges have a red or red and white streaked pulp. Hamlin is an excellent juice orange from Florida, available October to December.

Sour oranges are too tart to be eaten fresh. They are used for making marmalade and the peel is candied. The oil from sour oranges is used for food flavorings, in making liqueurs, or for medicinal and cosmetic purposes. Sour orange trees are grown in the Southeast or Southwest for ornamental purposes.

Mandarin oranges are loose-skinned, easily peeled and sectioned. Mandarin oranges are subdivided into tangerines, satsumas and miscellaneous hybrids which include tangelo and temple oranges. Florida and Mexico are the largest producers of mandarins, available from October to May. Japan is the largest producer of satsuma oranges, marketing them in December. Hybrid oranges are primarily grown in Florida.

To most people in this country and retailers as well, the term "tangerine" is used for all oranges that are zipper or slip-skinned. Tangerine is a type of mandarin; Clementine is a variety of tangerine. It is also called an Algerian tangerine. It is a medium to large fruit, with a red-orange, pebbled skin. Seed number varies from none to many. Dancy is a variety with a sweet-tart flavor and many seeds. A satsuma is a small to medium fruit. The rind is pebbled and orange; it is somewhat flattened and almost seedless. A tangelo is a grapefruit-tangerine hybrid. It resembles a tangerine with a red-orange skin. The pulp is fine-textured and tart. A temple orange is a cross between a tangerine and an orange. The fruit is large with a slightly rough, red-orange skin. The pulp is juicy, sweet and has noticeable seeds. Kinnow is another hybrid mandarin which is plentiful between January and May. It has a light orange, smooth rind, and a rich, sweet flavor with thin membranes around the segments, and many seeds.

Buying and Storing: Fresh oranges are available every month of the year, although the peak supply is December to March. Choose oranges that are heavy for their size. Skin color is not an indication of ripeness because some ripe oranges have a tinge of green. Some oranges are artificially dyed to improve their appearance. Such fruit must be stamped "color added." Oranges are sold by weight or piece.

Oranges will last at room temperature for up to a week. For best results, store in plastic bag or in the vegetable compartment of the refrigerator.

Orange segments are available in jars mixed with other fruits, and found refrigerated in supermarkets. Mandarin orange segments are available canned in heavy syrup.

Orange Nutrition: Oranges are an excellent source of vitamin C. A 2½-inch tangerine contains 46 calories; a 3½-inch navel orange contains 87 calories.

Orange Math
2 to 4 medium oranges = 1 cup juice
1 medium orange = 4 teaspoons grated rind
1 medium tangerine = 3 to 4 tablespoons juice or 2 to 3 teaspoons grated rind

CURRIED ORANGE RICE

Makes 6 servings.

- ¼ cup (½ stick) butter or margarine
- 1 medium-size onion, thinly sliced
- 2 teaspoons curry powder
- 1 cup uncooked long-grain rice
- 1 cup orange juice
- 1 cup chicken broth
- 1 teaspoon salt
- ½ cup raisins
- 1 bay leaf

1. Melt butter in a heavy saucepan or flameproof casserole; sauté onion until soft and golden, but not brown. Stir in curry and rice; cook 2 minutes longer, stirring constantly.

2. Add orange juice, chicken broth, salt, raisins and bay leaf; stir with fork. Bring to boiling; lower heat; cover; simmer 15 to 20 minutes or until rice is tender and liquid has been absorbed. Remove bay leaf before serving.

ORANGE GINGER SOY CHICKEN

Makes 8 servings.

- 2 broiler-fryers, about 3 pounds each, quartered
- 1 can (6 ounces) frozen orange juice concentrate, undiluted and thawed
- ⅓ cup dry sherry
- ⅓ cup soy sauce
- 1 teaspoon ground ginger
- 1 clove garlic, minced
- 1 teaspoon salt
- ¼ teaspoon pepper

1. Arrange chicken in shallow glass or enamel dish. Combine orange juice, sherry, soy sauce, ginger, garlic, salt and pepper in 4-cup measure. Pour orange mixture evenly over chicken. Marinate at least 2 hours at room temperature or in refrigerator overnight, turning chicken occasionally.

2. Drain chicken, reserving marinade. Place chicken, skin-side down, on rack of broiler pan. Broil 6 inches from heat for 40 minutes, turning often and brushing generously with reserved marinade, until chicken is fork-tender. Heat any remaining marinade to serve with chicken. Serve with hot rice.

Orange

CORNISH GAME HENS, FRENCH-STYLE

Bacon strips placed over the birds keeps them moist and oranges add a tart flavor.

Bake at 400° for 10 minutes, then at 350° for 1 hour.
Makes 4 servings.

- **4 Rock Cornish game hens (about ¾ to 1 pound each), thawed if frozen**
- **1 teaspoon salt**
- **½ teaspoon pepper**
- **1 small orange, cut into quarters and seeded**
- **4 bacon slices**
- **5 to 6 navel or Valencia oranges**
- **2 tablespoons butter or margarine**
- **¼ cup finely chopped shallots or green onion tops**
- **¼ cup red currant jelly**
- **1 teaspoon dry mustard**
- **¾ teaspoon salt**
- **½ teaspoon leaf tarragon, crumbled**
- **⅛ teaspoon cayenne**

1. Sprinkle inside of birds with salt and pepper; put 1 orange quarter into the cavity of each bird. Truss each bird by tying the legs and wings close to the body.
2. Cut bacon slices in half; cover the breast of each bird with two halves. Place the birds in a shallow roasting pan.
3. Bake in a hot oven (400°) for 10 minutes; lower oven temperature to moderate (350°); roast for an additional 45 minutes.
4. Grate rind from one orange (1 tablespoon). Cut orange rind from 2 more oranges with a vegetable parer or sharp knife (do not include white); cut rind into thin julienne strips. With a sharp knife, remove remaining white membrane from the 3 oranges over a large bowl to catch juice; then section.
5. Drain juice into a measuring cup. Squeeze juice from remaining oranges to make 1 cup orange juice; reserve.
6. Melt butter in a medium-size skillet; add shallots; cook until shal-

lots are soft but not browned. Stir in jelly and the orange rind, mustard, salt, tarragon and cayenne; cook until jelly is melted. Stir in orange juice; bring sauce to boiling.
7. Remove birds from oven; remove string and bacon. Carefully pour off all fat from roasting pan. Pour orange sauce over birds. Return to oven and bake an additional 15 minutes, basting frequently.
8. Remove from oven; place on heated serving platter. Place roasting pan on top of stove; bring sauce to boiling; add reserved orange sections and julienne orange strips; heat to boiling. Spoon a little sauce over each bird. Serve with remaining sauce. Garnish with parsley, if you wish.

TANGERINE AND CRANBERRY MOLD

Spoon the mixture into a relish dish instead of a mold, if you wish.

Makes 4 cups.

- **2 cups sugar**
- **1½ cups water**
- **4 cups fresh or frozen cranberries (about 1 pound)**
- **1 tangerine, peeled, seeded and finely chopped (⅔ cup)**
- **Leaf lettuce**

1. Combine sugar and water in medium-size saucepan; bring to boiling, stirring constantly. Boil, uncovered, for 5 minutes.
2. Add cranberries and tangerine. Cook 15 minutes until berries pop and mixture thickens slightly. Pour into a 4-cup mold or bowl; chill overnight.
3. To serve: Unmold onto serving plate. Garnish with lettuce and tangerine sections, if you wish.

ORANGE AVOCADO SALAD

Makes 6 servings.

- **1 medium-size head romaine**
- **3 large navel oranges**
- **1 large firm ripe avocado Lemon Dressing (recipe follows)**

1. Tear the romaine into bite-size pieces into a large salad bowl. Cut rind off oranges; section oranges into

a small bowl.
2. Just before serving, peel, pit and slice avocado. Arrange avocado and oranges over romaine. Drizzle ⅓ to ½ cup Lemon Dressing over salad; toss gently.

LEMON DRESSING

Makes ¾ cup.

- **¼ cup fresh lemon juice**
- **½ teaspoon salt**
- **⅛ teaspoon pepper**
- **¼ teaspoon sugar**
- **¼ teaspoon dry mustard**
- **½ cup vegetable oil**

1. Beat lemon juice, salt, pepper, sugar and dry mustard in a medium-size bowl.
2. Beat in the oil in a slow, steady stream; refrigerate. Stir well just before serving.

ORANGE WHOLE-WHEAT BREAD

Bake at 350° for 1 hour.
Makes 1 large loaf.

- **2 cups *sifted* all-purpose flour**
- **1 cup sugar**
- **3½ teaspoons baking powder**
- **1 teaspoon salt**
- **1 cup whole wheat flour**
- **¾ cup crunchy nut-like cereal nuggets**
- **1 egg**
- **4 teaspoons grated orange rind**
- **¾ cup orange juice**
- **¾ cup milk**
- **¼ cup (½ stick) butter, melted**

1. Sift all-purpose flour, sugar, baking powder and salt into a large bowl. Stir in whole wheat flour and cereal nuggets. Preheat oven to 350°.
2. Beat egg in a small bowl. Stir in orange rind and juice, milk and butter.
3. Pour liquid ingredients into dry ingredients and stir just until moist. Spoon batter into greased 9×5×3-inch loaf pan.
4. Bake in a preheated moderate oven (350°) for 1 hour or until a wooden pick inserted in the center comes out clean. Cool in pan on wire rack 10 minutes. Remove from pan; cool completely. Wrap in foil when cool; store overnight.

Pictured opposite: (Clockwise from top right) Glacéed Oranges, page 472; Orange Soufflé, page 472; Curried Orange Rice, page 469; Cornish Game Hens, French-Style, page 470; Thailand Stuffed Oranges, page 472.

Orange

GLACÉED ORANGES

Bright slivers of candied orange peel and a touch of orange-flavored liqueur add zest to this simple dessert.

Makes 6 servings.

- **6 large navel oranges**
- **2 cups sugar**
- **1 cup water**
- **2 tablespoons orange-flavored liqueur**

1. Remove thin, bright-colored rind (no white) from each orange with a vegetable parer or sharp knife; cut into thin strips; reserve.
2. Simmer rind in 4 cups boiling water for 8 minutes; drain and reserve the rind.
3. With a sharp knife, cut remaining white membrane from oranges. Remove core from center of orange. Place oranges in a bowl just large enough to hold them.
4. Combine sugar with water in a heavy saucepan; cook over medium heat, stirring constantly, until sugar is dissolved. Continue cooking without stirring until mixture is syrupy, about 10 minutes. Add blanched orange rind; cook about 5 minutes or until rind becomes translucent. Remove from heat; add orange liqueur. Pour hot syrup with rind over oranges. Cool; chill several hours or overnight. Garnish each orange with candied violets if you wish.

ORANGE SHERBET IN ORANGE CUPS

A most appealing and attractive dessert.

Makes 8 servings.

- **8 navel or Valencia oranges**
- **1 envelope unflavored gelatin**
- **1¼ cups sugar**
- **1 cup milk**
- **¼ cup ground blanched almonds**
- **3 tablespoons orange-flavored liqueur**
- **1 teaspoon almond extract**
- **2 egg whites**

1. Cut oranges in half; squeeze and strain juice. Measure and reserve 2¾ cups of the juice. Remove crushed pulp from 8 of the orange shells for serving cups; scallop edges with a paring knife. Wrap in foil or plastic; refrigerate.
2. Combine gelatin and 1 cup of the sugar in a medium-size saucepan. Stir in 1½ cups of the orange juice. Heat, stirring constantly, until mixture just comes to boiling. Lower heat; simmer, stirring occasionally, 5 minutes.
3. Remove from heat; cool. Stir in remaining orange juice and the milk, almonds, orange liqueur and almond extract. (Mixture will look curdled.) Pour into a 13 × 9 × 2-inch metal pan. Freeze until mixture is almost solidly frozen, about 4 hours.
4. Beat egg whites in a small bowl with electric mixer until foamy. Gradually beat in remaining ¼ cup sugar until meringue forms soft peaks.
5. Break up frozen mixture into chunks; turn into chilled large bowl. Beat with electric mixer until smooth. Quickly fold in meringue. Cover with foil; freeze overnight.
6. To serve: Spoon frozen sherbet into reserved orange shells.

ORANGE SOUFFLÉ

Makes 6 servings.

- **1 envelope unflavored gelatin**
- **¼ cup water**
- **3 eggs, separated**
- **½ cup sugar**
- **2 tablespoons grated orange rind**
- **¾ cup fresh orange juice**
- **1 tablespoon lemon juice**
- **1 cup heavy cream**

1. Prepare a 1-quart soufflé dish with a collar. Sprinkle gelatin over water in a small saucepan; let stand to soften, 10 minutes. Place saucepan over very low heat until gelatin dissolves, 2 or 3 minutes (mixture will be clear). Remove; cool.
2. Beat the egg yolks until light in large bowl of electric mixer. Add sugar, 2 tablespoons at a time, and beat until mixture becomes thick and light. Add orange rind, orange and lemon juices.
3. Combine cooled gelatin with egg yolk mixture. Place bowl in a larger bowl partly filled with ice and water. Stir frequently just until mixture is thick enough to mound.
4. Beat egg whites in a small bowl until firm peaks form. Beat heavy cream in another small bowl until soft peaks form.
5. Fold in egg whites and heavy cream with a rubber spatula until no streaks of white remain. Pour into prepared dish. Refrigerate 3 hours or until set. Remove collar. Garnish with additional heavy cream and orange slices, if you wish.

MANDARIN ORANGE SAUCE

Makes 2 cups.

- **⅓ cup sugar**
- **2 tablespoons cornstarch**
- **1 can (11 ounces) mandarin oranges**
- **½ cup orange juice**

1. Combine sugar and cornstarch in a medium-size saucepan.
2. Drain syrup from mandarin oranges into saucepan; add orange juice. Heat to boiling, stirring constantly, until thickened; add drained oranges.

THAILAND STUFFED ORANGES

Bake at 300° for 30 minutes.
Makes 6 servings.

- **6 large navel oranges**
- **2 tablespoons vegetable oil**
- **1 clove garlic, minced**
- **1½ pounds lean ground pork**
- **⅓ cup chopped unsalted peanuts**
- **1 teaspoon salt**
- **½ teaspoon crushed red pepper**
- **¼ teaspoon ground coriander**
- **2 teaspoons anchovy paste**
- **2 tablespoons flour**
  Watercress

1. Cut off top of each orange ⅓ of the way down; cut a thin slice off the bottom of each orange so that they will stand firmly.
2. With a sharp paring knife or grapefruit knife and holding over a pie plate, cut inside about ⅛ inch from orange shell and down, rotating knife so that the inside pulp comes out in a cone-shaped piece. Cut off a ½-inch thick piece for garnish; reserve. With a spoon, scrape out excess juice, but do not scrape out remaining orange. Pour juice through

strainer into a 2-cup liquid measuring cup; squeeze enough of the pulp into the cup to equal 1½ cups. Coarsely chop remaining orange pulp; reserve both.

3. Heat oil in large skillet; add garlic and cook just until brown. Add pork, peanuts, salt, red pepper, coriander and anchovy paste, mixing thoroughly. Cook over medium heat for 15 minutes, stirring frequently.

4. Drain off any fat. Stir in flour to coat meat. Add orange juice; cook, stirring constantly, until mixture thickens; add coarsely chopped orange pulp.

5. Fill orange shells with meat mixture, mounding slightly. Place stuffed oranges in a shallow baking pan.

6. Bake in a slow oven (300°) for 30 minutes or until stuffing is piping hot. Transfer to heated serving platter and garnish with reserved orange pieces and watercress.

CAKE A L'ORANGE

Fragrant with fresh oranges, this cake needs no frosting.

Bake at 350° for 50 minutes.
Makes one 9-inch tube cake.

    2 cups *sifted* all-purpose flour
    1 teaspoon baking powder
    1 teaspoon baking soda
    1 cup (2 sticks) butter or
      margarine, softened
 1½ cups sugar
    3 eggs, separated
    1 container (8 ounces) dairy sour
      cream
    1 tablespoon grated orange rind
    ½ cup chopped walnuts or
      pecans
    ¼ cup orange juice
    ⅓ cup Grand Marnier or other
      orange-flavored liqueur
    2 tablespoons chopped nuts

1. Sift flour, baking powder and baking soda onto wax paper.

2. Preheat oven to 350°. Beat butter, 1 cup of the sugar and egg yolks in a large bowl until light and fluffy.

3. Add flour mixture alternately with sour cream, starting and ending with flour. Stir in orange rind and the ½ cup chopped walnuts or pecans.

4. Beat egg whites in a small bowl

with electric mixer until stiff but not dry; fold into batter. Spoon batter into a greased 9-inch tube pan.

5. Bake in a preheated moderate oven (350°) for 50 minutes or until a wooden pick inserted in top comes out clean.

6. Combine orange juice and remaining ½ cup sugar in a small saucepan. Heat, stirring constantly, over low heat just until sugar is dissolved. Remove from heat and stir in Grand Marnier. Spoon mixture over hot cake. Sprinkle with 2 tablespoons nuts. Cool in pan on wire rack 15 minutes; loosen around edge and tube with knife; turn out onto wire rack; cool completely.

———— ●●● ————

OREGANO An aromatic plant of the mint family and closely related to marjoram. Oregano is believed to be native to the Mediterranean region. The leaves are grayish-green and oval. Fresh oregano is available in local markets in season. More commonly, oregano is available as crumbled, dried leaves. Oregano is highly esteemed as a seasoning for Italian, Spanish and Mexican dishes. Use oregano in sauces, soups and stews. See also **HERBS**.

ORZO A pasta shaped like large grains of rice. Prepare it according to package directions or as indicated in the recipe.

OXTAIL See **VARIETY MEAT**.

OYSTER A bivalve mollusk found in shallow waters along the coasts of many continents. Oysters are usually identified by locality. The most common are known as Blue Points, cultured in Long Island, but the same species is also called Cape Cod, Chincoteague, Kent Island, etc. Blue Point oysters are 2 to 4 inches long and about 2½ inches wide. Many famous varieties are harvested from the Chesapeake Bay, with Maryland the largest oyster producer in the country. Oysters native to the Pacific coast include the small Olympia, rarely more than 2 inches long, and the

large Pacific or Japanese oysters which grow up to 12 inches long. Oysters are also harvested from Louisiana, Mississippi and Florida coasts.

Buying and Storing: In large communities, oysters are sold live in the shell and are at their best in the fall and winter months. They are sold by the dozen. Allow 6 oysters per appetizer serving. Choose only oysters with tightly closed shells. Keep refrigerated, then shuck and serve or cook as soon as possible.

Freshly shucked oysters are also available sold in containers, refrigerated, iced or frozen. Eastern oysters are graded by sizes. "Counts" are extra-large oysters or about 44 per quart. "Extra-selects" are large or about 50 per quart. "Selects" are medium or about 75 oysters per quart. These are ideal for frying. "Standards" are very small oysters and should be used for stews or chowders. Shucked oysters should be odorless, with the liquor clear and free of shell particles. Keep refrigerated and cook as soon as possible.

Oysters are also marketed cooked and packaged in cans, smoked and canned, and sun-dried imported from the Far East.

OYSTER STEW

Makes 4 servings.

    2 cups milk
    2 cups light cream or
      half-and-half
    ½ teaspoon salt
    ¼ teaspoon paprika
    1 pint (about 24) shucked oysters
      with liquor
      OR: 2 cans (8 ounces each)
      oysters
    ¼ cup (½ stick) butter or
      margarine

1. Scald milk with cream in medium-size saucepan over low heat, but do not boil; stir in salt and paprika.

2. Heat oysters and their liquor in butter until edges of oysters begin to curl in medium-size saucepan; stir in milk mixture.

3. Ladle into soup bowls. Serve with oyster crackers, if you wish.

Oyster Plant

OYSTERS ROCKEFELLER

This appetizer was invented at Antoine's, the famous New Orleans restaurant, by Jules Alciatore in the 1850's.

Makes 6 servings.

  6 tablespoons (¾ stick) butter or margarine
  ½ cup packaged bread crumbs
  2 cups fresh spinach leaves, washed and stemmed
  ½ cup parsley sprigs
  ½ cup diced celery
  2 tablespoons diced onion
  1 tablespoon Pernod liqueur
  ¼ teaspoon salt
  3 drops liquid hot pepper seasoning
 18 large oysters on the half shell (*See Note*)
    Rock salt

1. Melt butter in a small saucepan; add bread crumbs; sauté for 1 minute. Remove from heat.
2. Combine buttered crumbs, spinach, parsley, celery, onion, Pernod, salt and pepper seasoning in container of an electric blender. Cover and whirl, stopping to stir contents several times, until the mixture is smooth. Pour into a small bowl; refrigerate until ready to use.
3. Arrange oysters in shells on a bed of rock salt in six individual, heatproof dishes, placing 3 in each dish. (Rock salt steadies oyster shells and retains heat.) Top each oyster with a tablespoonful of the spinach mixture.
4. Broil 4 inches from heat for 3 minutes or just until topping is lightly browned and heated through. Serve at once.
Note: If oysters in the shell are not available, place well-drained shucked oysters in scallop shells or in small, heatproof serving dishes. Add topping and broil as above.

NEW ENGLAND OYSTER SCALLOP

Oysters bake plump and moist between layers of buttery crumbs.

Bake at 350° for 30 minutes.
Makes 4 to 6 servings.

  ¼ cup (½ stick) butter or margarine
  2 cups coarse soda-cracker crumbs (about 24 crackers)
  ½ cup chopped fresh parsley
  1 teaspoon salt
  ¼ teaspoon pepper
  1 pint (about 24) shucked oysters with liquor
    OR: 2 cans (8 ounces each) oysters
  ½ cup light cream
  1 teaspoon Worcestershire sauce

1. Melt the butter in a saucepan; remove from heat; stir in crumbs, parsley, salt and pepper.
2. Drain and save ¼ cup liquor from oysters. Sprinkle ⅓ of crumb mixture into a 9-inch pie plate; layer half of the oysters on top, then half of remaining crumbs and rest of oysters.
3. Combine reserved oyster liquor, cream and Worcestershire sauce; pour over the top; sprinkle with remaining crumbs.
4. Bake in a moderate oven (350°) for 30 minutes or until top is golden. Serve hot, plain or with chili sauce.

OYSTER SANDWICH

Makes 6 sandwiches.

  1 medium-size tomato, diced (about 1 cup)
  ⅓ cup diced green pepper
  ⅓ cup chopped green onions
  ½ teaspoon leaf basil, crumbled
  ¼ cup bottled oil and vinegar salad dressing
  6 individual hero rolls
  ¼ cup (½ stick) butter or margarine, melted
  ¼ cup all-purpose flour
  2 eggs
  ½ teaspoon salt
  ⅛ teaspoon cayenne
  1 pint (about 24) shucked oysters, drained
    OR: 2 cans (8 ounces each) oysters
    Vegetable oil for frying

1. Combine tomato, green pepper, onions, basil and dressing in a small bowl. Cover; refrigerate.
2. Cut each roll lengthwise about ⅓ down, but do not cut top off. Scoop out doughy bread from bottom half; crumble into crumbs. Place 1½ cups on wax paper. (Save remainder for other use.) Brush inside of rolls with melted butter; place on cookie sheet.
3. Place flour on another piece of wax paper. Beat eggs, salt and cayenne in a pie plate.
4. Coat oysters with flour; dip into egg mixture; coat with crumbs. Refrigerate 15 minutes.
5. Heat rolls in a moderate oven (350°) for 12 minutes.
6. Heat 1½ inches oil in a large saucepan to 375° on a deep-fat frying thermometer. Fry oysters, 1 layer deep, until golden. Drain on paper toweling.
7. To serve: Spoon some tomato-pepper mixture in bottom of each roll. Top with 3 or 4 fried oysters. Cover sandwich and serve with lemon wedges, if you wish.

— ●●● —

OYSTER PLANT Also called salsify and vegetable oyster, this winter vegetable is a root which tastes somewhat like an oyster. The root is similar in appearance to parsnips except the tops of the plant look like thick grass. The plant, a member of the sunflower family, is native to southern Europe.
Buying and Storing: Available from June to March; look for firm roots about 10 inches long, sold in bunches. One pound makes about 3 servings. Store in the refrigerator and use within 4 days.
To Prepare: Oyster plant discolors when cut so have a bowl of acidulated water ready (1 tablespoon vinegar or lemon juice added to 1 quart water). Trim off ends and scrape the roots. Wash, drain and cut into slices or sticks. Drop into acidulated water until ready to cook. Drain before cooking.
To Cook: Add a tablespoon lemon juice to an inch of boiling water in a saucepan. Add cut-up oyster plant. Cover and cook over low heat 5 to 10 minutes or until just tender. Drain and season with butter or a cream sauce. Or, add a clear salad dressing and marinate cooked oyster plant in the refrigerator until cold.

PAELLA A popular Spanish one-dish meal containing rice, chicken, shellfish and vegetables cooked and served in a special shallow metal cooking pan. Saffron is the dominant seasoning.

PAELLA

A classic that's not as complicated as it may seem.

Bake at 350° for 1 hour.
Makes 8 to 10 servings.

- 1 **broiler-fryer (2½ to 3 pounds), cut up**
- 2 **tablespoons flour**
- ¼ **cup olive or vegetable oil**
- 1½ **cups uncooked long-grain rice**
- 1 **large onion, chopped (1 cup)**
- 1 **clove garlic, minced**
- 1 **small green pepper, seeded and chopped**
- 1 **canned pimiento, cut into strips**
- 1 **pound fresh peas, shelled (1 cup)**
  - OR: **1 cup frozen peas**
- 4 **tomatoes, peeled and sliced**
- 1 **bottle (8 ounces) clam juice**
- 1½ **cups water**
- 1 **teaspoon or envelope instant chicken broth**
- ½ **teaspoon salt**
- ¼ **teaspoon pepper**
- ¼ **teaspoon saffron threads, crushed**
- 2 **cans (8 ounces each) minced clams** *(See Note)*
- 1 **pound fresh or frozen shrimp, shelled and deveined**

Coat chicken pieces with flour; brown in oil in large skillet; place in a 12-cup baking dish or paella pan.
2. Sauté rice, onion, garlic, green pepper and pimiento in oil in same skillet, stirring often, 10 minutes or until rice is golden; spoon over and around the chicken in the baking dish; top with peas and tomatoes.
3. Combine clam juice, water, instant chicken broth, salt, pepper and saffron in the same skillet and bring to boiling; pour over mixture in baking dish; cover.
4. Bake in a moderate oven (350°) for 30 minutes; add clams and liquid and shrimp; cover; bake 30 minutes longer or until chicken is tender.
Note: If fresh mussels or clams are available, buy 12 to 18 and use them in place of canned minced clams. To cook: Scrub shells well; place in large saucepan with 1 cup water; cover; bring to boiling; simmer 3 to 5 minutes or until shells open. Lift out with tongs. Strain broth through cheesecloth to remove any sand; measure (you should have 1 cup). Substitute for bottled clam juice in Step 3. Use mussels in shells in place of minced clams in Step 4. Place with shrimp on top of paella.

● ● ●

PANCAKE One of the oldest forms of bread, a pancake is a flat cake cooked or baked on a griddle. The first pancakes were probably made of ground meal and water and spread on a hot stone to dry. Almost every country has their own version of a pancake. Pancakes can be served as an appetizer, stuffed and served as a main dish or as dessert.

Tips for Perfect Pancakes
1. Make sure your griddle is hot before adding the batter. Here's how to test it: Sprinkle on several drops of water; when they sputter and dance about, grease griddle and pour the pancake batter.
2. For equal-size pancakes, measure batter, using a scant ¼ cup for a 4-inch round. The batter spreads, so leave space between cakes.
3. When pancakes look puffy and golden on the undersides, flip them over with a wide spatula.

APPLE PANCAKES

Makes about 24 two-inch pancakes.

- 1 **cup** *unsifted* **all-purpose flour**
- ½ **teaspoon baking powder**
- ½ **cup milk***
- 2 **eggs, lightly beaten**
- 3 **small McIntosh apples, pared, quartered, cored and chopped**
- 1 **tablespoon vegetable oil**

1. Mix flour and baking powder in a medium-size bowl; stir in milk and

eggs until batter is smooth. Fold in chopped apples.

2. Heat oil in a large skillet. For each pancake, drop a heaping tablespoon of batter in the skillet. Cook until golden brown on bottom; turn; cook until golden on the other side. Serve with butter and honey or syrup, if you wish.

If batter is too thick, stir in more milk.

PANCAKES WITH ORANGE-HONEY BUTTER

Makes about 40 three-inch pancakes or 8 servings.

- 1¾ cups *sifted* all-purpose flour
- 1 teaspoon baking powder
- ½ teaspoon salt
- 3 eggs
- 1 tablespoon honey
- 1½ cups buttermilk
- 1 teaspoon baking soda
- 3 tablespoons vegetable oil
  Orange-Honey Butter *(recipe follows)*

1. Sift flour, baking powder and salt onto wax paper.
2. Beat eggs and honey in a medium-size bowl; stir in buttermilk and baking soda.
3. Add sifted dry ingredients and oil to the egg mixture and beat until smooth.
4. Drop batter by tablespoonfuls onto a lightly greased, medium-hot griddle. Brown pancakes; turn and cook other side. Serve with Orange-Honey Butter.

Orange-Honey Butter: Beat ½ cup (1 stick) softened butter or margarine, ⅓ cup honey and 2 tablespoons thawed, undiluted, frozen orange juice concentrate in a medium-size bowl until mixture is light and fluffy. Makes about 1 cup.

CHEESE PANCAKES WITH PEAR SAUCE

Makes about 9 four-inch pancakes or 3 servings.

- 1 can (16 ounces) pear slices
- 1 tablespoon minced crystallized ginger
- 1 teaspoon cornstarch
- 1 tablespoon butter or margarine

- 1 container (8 ounces) cottage cheese
- 1 cup water
- 1¼ cups complete pancake mix
  Melted butter or vegetable oil for frying

1. Drain pears, reserving ¼ cup syrup. Combine pears, syrup, ginger and cornstarch in a medium-size saucepan. Cook over medium heat until thickened and bubbly. Stir in butter; keep warm.
2. Combine cottage cheese and water in container of electric blender or food processor. Cover; whirl until smooth. Stir in pancake mix.
3. Heat griddle or large skillet. Brush generously with butter or oil. Pour batter until 4-inch pancake forms. Cook until golden brown; turn and cook until firm. Serve with sauce.

SOUR CREAM POTATO PANCAKES

Makes about 2½ dozen pancakes.

- 2 pounds baking potatoes (about 3 large)
- 2 eggs
- 1 small onion, grated (¼ cup)
- 1 container (8 ounces) dairy sour cream
- ½ cup *sifted* all-purpose flour
- ¼ teaspoon baking powder
- 1 teaspoon salt
- ¼ teaspoon white pepper
  Vegetable oil for frying

1. Pare potatoes; shred coarsely into a large bowl of cold water. Drain, then rinse in cold running water. Squeeze firmly in clean linen toweling or cheesecloth to remove as much water as possible.
2. Beat eggs in a large bowl until frothy. Add potatoes, onion, sour cream, flour, baking powder, salt and pepper; stir.
3. Heat a ¼-inch depth of oil in a large skillet. Drop potato mixture by tablespoonfuls into hot oil (add more oil as needed); flatten with pancake turner to make an even thickness. Brown on one side (about 5 to 6 minutes); turn and brown other side. Drain on paper toweling. Serve warm.

— ●●● —

Papaya

PAPAYA A greenish-yellow, oval fruit with soft golden-pink flesh, papaya grows on a subtropical tree. The average size is about 6 inches long and 3 inches wide. Some varieties weigh up to 20 pounds. Most are grown in Hawaii, Puerto Rico, Florida and southern California. Papaya is also called *pawpaw*. Papaya is usually eaten when ripe as dessert or used in salads, pies or made into sherbet or ice cream. Unripe or green papaya can be cooked as a vegetable and tastes somewhat like squash. Half-ripe papaya is a source of papain, an enzyme which is used in meat tenderizers. Ripe papaya has little or no papain present.

Papaya is an excellent source of vitamins A and C. A 3½-ounce serving contains 39 calories. The numerous tiny black seeds inside a papaya are edible. They are considered an aid to digestion and are eaten by people living in papaya-growing areas. You can put them in a blender or food processor and whirl until finely ground, then add them to a fruit salad dressing.

Buying and Storing: Papaya is available year-round with the best supplies in late winter and early spring. The fruit is picked firm and will ripen in 3 to 5 days at room temperature. Select firm, mostly yellow fruit with no bruises or soft spots. Store ripe papaya in the refrigerator.

PAPAYA SALAD WITH FRUIT DRESSING

Makes 4 servings.

- 1 large papaya
  Lettuce leaves
- 2 tablespoons vegetable oil
- 3 tablespoons orange juice
- 1 teaspoon lemon juice
- 1 large banana
- 1 cup halved seedless green grapes

Pare, quarter and seed papaya. Arrange on 4 lettuce-lined salad plates. Combine oil, orange juice and lemon juice in a bowl. Slice banana into dressing; spoon over papaya. Garnish with grape halves.

Papaya

FROZEN PAPAYA CREAM

Simple to make and so good! Serve it alone or with fragrant ripe strawberries or peaches.

Makes about 1 quart.

   2 medium-size papayas
   ¼ cup lemon juice
   ½ cup sugar
   1 cup light cream or half-and-half

1. Cut papayas in half lengthwise; scoop out and discard seeds; then scoop out pulp (about 2 cups). Puree papaya with lemon juice and sugar in container of an electric blender or food processor until smooth. Stir in cream. Pour mixture into a 9 × 9 × 2-inch pan.

2. Place in freezer 1 hour or until frozen 1 inch in from edges. Stir with a spoon until smooth. Return to freezer another 30 minutes to 1 hour or until softly frozen. Spoon into chilled medium-size bowl; beat with electric mixer until smooth, 1 to 2 minutes. Spoon into plastic container or bowl; cover. Freeze until firm, about 6 hours or overnight.

───────── ● ●● ─────────

PAPRIKA

PAPRIKA A spice used as a seasoning and a garnish. Paprika is made by grinding the dried pods of *Capsicum* or sweet red pepper. The imported Spanish paprika used in the United States is mild. Some paprika is produced in southern California, central Europe and, of course, Hungary. Paprika, a Hungarian word, is essential in many Hungarian dishes. The pungency, quality, color and flavor of paprika depend on the variety of peppers used and the method of processing. The pungent varieties are available in specialty stores. Store paprika in an airtight container in a cool, dry place or refrigerate. Use in soups, stews and cream sauces.

CHICKEN PAPRIKA WITH SPATZLE

Paprika-flavored chicken in sour cream sauce, served with tender homemade dumplings.

Makes 6 servings.

   1 broiler-fryer (3 to 3½ pounds), cut up
   ½ cup all-purpose flour
   1½ teaspoons salt
   ¼ teaspoon pepper
   ½ cup (1 stick) butter or margarine
   1 large onion, chopped (1 cup)
   2 tablespoons paprika
   1 cup chicken broth
   1 cup light cream or half-and-half
   ½ cup dairy sour cream
     Spatzle *(recipe follows)*

1. Shake chicken in plastic bag with flour, 1 teaspoon of the salt and pepper until coated. Reserve 2 tablespoons of the flour mixture.

2. Brown chicken in butter in a large skillet, removing pieces as they brown to plate. Pour pan fat into a measuring cup. Return 3 tablespoons to skillet.

3. Sauté onion in fat until light golden brown, about 10 minutes. Add paprika, remaining ½ teaspoon salt and chicken broth. Bring to boiling; lower heat; return chicken, turning to coat. Cook, covered, 30 minutes or until chicken is tender. Remove chicken; keep warm.

4. Stir in light cream. Make a paste of the reserved 2 tablespoons flour mixture and sour cream; slowly stir into skillet. Cook, stirring constantly, over low heat until thickened. *Do not boil.* Return chicken. Serve over Spatzle. Sprinkle with chopped parsley, if you wish.

SPATZLE

Makes 6 servings.

   3 cups *sifted* all-purpose flour
   1 teaspoon salt
   ⅛ teaspoon white pepper
   3 eggs, slightly beaten
   1 cup water
   ¼ cup (½ stick) butter or margarine, melted

1. Combine flour, salt and pepper in a medium-size bowl; make well in center. Add eggs and water to well and mix thoroughly.

2. Scoop up dough on a spatula and cut off small pieces with knife into boiling salted water. As spatzle rises to the top, remove with slotted spoon and put in covered bowl until all are made. Toss with butter; keep warm.

───────── ● ●● ─────────

PARMESAN CHEESE An excellent and well known cheese originating in Italy in the 1200's. Parmesan is named for a small region in Italy called Parma. It is made from whole cow's milk. When fresh, Parmesan can be sliced for eating, but it is best known as a hard, aged cheese which must be grated before use. When aged, it has a sharp, pungent flavor. The Parmesan cheese sold already grated in jars or cans bears little resemblance to freshly grated Parmesan. Fresh Parmesan is made in the United States and is also imported from Italy.

PARSLEY An herb used as a flavoring and a garnish. Parsley is a member of the *Umbelliferae* or umbel family which includes anise, dill, chervil, celery and carrots. Parsley varieties are distinguished by the shape of the leaves. The two most common types are the curly and flat or Italian parsley.

Parsley is sold fresh in bunches year-round, or as dried flakes. See also **HERBS**.

PARSNIP A root vegetable harvested after the first frost, parsnips look like ivory-colored carrots. Parsnips are a member of the *Umbelliferae* or umbel family which also includes carrots, parsley, celery and other herbs. It is native to the eastern Mediterranean area.

Parsnips can be served as a cooked vegetable or added to soups and stews.

Buying and Storing: The peak growing season is September through May. Buy small to medium roots; large roots tend to be woody. Purchase ¼ to ⅓ pound for a serving. Store refrigerated in plastic bags. They will keep several weeks.

To Prepare and Cook: Trim, peel and wash parsnips. Cut in slices, sticks or cubes. Cook pieces in an inch of boiling water for 5 to 10 minutes. Drain; season with butter, salt and pepper. Or, drain and mash parsnips. Parsnips can also be braised in broth or deep-fat fried.

GLAZED PARSNIPS

These glazed parsnips are excellent with roast meat.

Makes 4 servings.

- 1 **pound parsnips (6 medium-size)**
- 3 **tablespoons butter or margarine**
- ¼ **cup firmly packed brown sugar**
- ¼ **teaspoon salt**
- ¼ **cup cider vinegar**
- 3 **tablespoons orange juice**

1. Cook unpared parsnips in boiling salted water to cover in a large saucepan for 10 minutes. Lower heat; simmer 20 minutes longer or until tender but firm. Remove skins while hot; cut parsnips into quarters.
2. Melt butter in a large skillet; stir in sugar, salt, vinegar and orange juice; bring to boiling. Add parsnips and cook over high heat, spooning pan liquid over, about 5 minutes or until well-glazed.

BREADED PARSNIPS

Makes 4 servings.

- 1 **pound parsnips**
- 2 **eggs, slightly beaten**
- ⅔ **cup packaged bread crumbs (seasoned or plain)**
- ½ **cup (1 stick) butter or margarine**

1. Pare parsnips; cut lengthwise into quarters, and then into 3-inch sticks.
2. Cook, covered, in boiling salted water in a large saucepan until almost tender, about 10 minutes; drain. Dip each piece in egg then roll in crumbs.
3. Heat butter in large skillet. Sauté parsnips, turning once or twice, until tender and golden brown on all sides.

• • •

PASSION FRUIT The egg-shaped, purple fruit of a vine native to South America and now grown in California and Australia. Passion fruit is also called granadilla. The flesh is yellow with tiny black seeds. It is eaten as a table fruit or used for making cakes, jellies or nectar.

Passion fruit is so named because early Christian missionaries to South America, upon seeing the flower of the fruit, thought it as symbolic of the crown of thorns of Christ.

There are two lesser known species of passion fruit. One is the sweet granadilla, oval-shaped and 3 to 6 inches long with an orange-brown leathery skin. The pulp is translucent and white. The other species is a giant granadilla which grows up to 10 inches long with a greenish-yellow skin. The pulp is purplish, sweetly acidic and mixed with flat seeds.

Passion fruit is available in some markets during the fall. Canned passion fruit nectar is sold in the gourmet section of the supermarket.

PASTA An Italian term used for the products of a paste made from semolina—milled from durum wheat—and water. Italians have taken the paste or dough and shaped it over 150 ways. Pasta is usually divided into the following types:

Macaroni — A tubular pasta. It can be long rods, short thick tubes, bent into elbow macaroni, and shaped into shells or curls.

Spaghetti — Solid strands of round, flat or curly pasta. Very thin strands are called *capelletti d'angelo* (angel's hair).

Noodles — These are ribbons of dough which may be cut into different widths or shapes. Most noodles are made with eggs added to the dough. Noodles can be flavored or colored with vegetables such as spinach, carrots or tomatoes.

How much pasta should you cook and serve? It's a matter of personal preference. One pound of spaghetti is sufficient for 6 to 8 first course or accompaniment servings but makes only 3 to 4 main-dish servings.

Different shapes of pasta are interchangeable in most recipes but if the size or thickness is different, the amount of pasta needed may have to be adjusted. Dry or uncooked pasta should be substituted by weight, not measurement, because pastas of different shapes will not have the same volume. A cupful of one pasta may differ in weight from a cupful of a differently shaped pasta. Cooked pasta can be substituted cup for cup.

Although dried pasta is widely available in packages, many stores in large cities are carrying freshly-made pasta. Some types of pasta can easily be made at home with the aid of a pasta machine. Depending on the model, a pasta machine can either make noodles only or some can also make shaped pasta. A noodle machine rolls dough between rollers and then cuts it into strips. A pasta maker is equipped with different discs for shaping dough. Electric pasta machines can make numerous pasta products.

For more recipes and information, see also **MACARONI, NOODLES, SPAGHETTI.**

How to Cook Pasta

1. Use a large kettle because the pasta needs plenty of room to bubble if it's to cook without sticking.
2. Do not cook more than 1 pound of pasta at a time in the same kettle. It will clump or stick together.
3. Fill a large kettle with water, leaving about 4 inches at the top (for 1 pound of pasta, you should use at least 12 cups of water). Add a drop of olive or vegetable oil (this helps keep pasta from sticking), set kettle over high heat and bring to a boil. Salt the cooking water or not.
4. When cooking long macaroni or spaghetti, slowly lower a handful at a time into the rapidly boiling water until it softens enough to fit into the kettle. Stir once or twice to separate strands, if necessary.
5. Boil rapidly, uncovered, until a strand of pasta cut in half shows no raw starch in the center—it shows up as a white dot—or until the pasta has no raw starch taste, but *does* feel a bit firm between the teeth (*al dente* is the Italian term for this firm-tenderness).
6. Drain pasta in a large colander the instant it's *al dente.* But do not rinse in cool water unless the pasta is for a salad.
7. If pasta must wait a few minutes before being served, toss with a little oil, set the colander over a kettle containing about 1 inch of simmering water and cover.

Pasta

SPAGHETTI WITH MEAT SAUCE

Makes 4 servings.

- 2 tablespoons olive or vegetable oil
- 1 medium-size onion, chopped (½ cup)
- 1 clove garlic, minced
- 1 pound ground beef or chuck
- 1 can (35 ounces) plum tomatoes
- 1 can (6 ounces) tomato paste
- ½ cup water
- ¼ cup chopped celery
- 2 tablespoons chopped fresh parsley
- 1 bay leaf
- 1 teaspoon leaf basil, crumbled
- 1 teaspoon salt
- 1 teaspoon sugar
- ⅛ teaspoon pepper
- 1 package (16 ounces) spaghetti Grated Parmesan cheese

1. Heat oil in a large saucepan. Add onion and garlic; sauté just until onion is soft; push to one side.
2. Add ground beef; cook until well browned, breaking up into chunks. Stir in tomatoes, tomato paste, water, celery, parsley, bay leaf, basil, salt, sugar and pepper.
3. Bring to boiling; partially cover and simmer, stirring several times, 1 hour or until sauce is thick. Skim off any fat; remove bay leaf.
4. Cook spaghetti following label directions; drain.
5. Spoon cooked spaghetti and meat sauce onto individual plates. Toss and serve with grated Parmesan cheese.

FUSILLI WITH SPINACH PESTO

A year-round version of classic pesto.

Makes 4 servings.

- 5 cups fresh spinach leaves (about ½ pound untrimmed), washed and thoroughly drained
- 1 package (16 ounces) fusilli, spaghetti or linguine
- 2 tablespoons olive or vegetable oil
- 1 large clove garlic
- ½ teaspoon salt
- ¼ teaspoon pepper
- 1 teaspoon leaf basil

- ¼ cup walnuts
- 1 cup ricotta cheese
- 2 tablespoons freshly grated Parmesan cheese

1. Remove and discard all tough woody stems from spinach.
2. Cook pasta following label directions.
3. Place the oil, garlic, salt and pepper in container of electric blender or food processor. Cover and whirl until garlic is pureed. Add basil and walnuts and whirl again until nuts are finely ground. Add cheeses; whirl until smooth. Start adding spinach leaves, 1 cup at a time, and whirl until smooth. Between additions, scrape mixture down side of container with a rubber spatula.
4. To serve: Stir about 3 tablespoonfuls of the hot pasta cooking water into sauce. Drain pasta and return to kettle. Add sauce and toss.

SPAGHETTI WITH BROCCOLI, TOMATOES AND WALNUTS

Makes 4 servings.

- 1 package (16 ounces) thin spaghetti or linguine
- ¼ cup (½ stick) butter or margarine
- 2 tablespoons olive or vegetable oil
- ½ cup coarsely chopped walnuts
- 1 pint cherry tomatoes, stems removed
- 1 large clove garlic, minced
- ½ teaspoon salt
  Pinch crushed red pepper
- 1 teaspoon leaf basil, crumbled
- 1 medium-size bunch broccoli, cut into 1-inch pieces (about 6 cups)
- ½ to 1 cup chicken broth
- ½ cup grated Parmesan cheese
- ¼ cup chopped fresh parsley

1. Cook pasta following label directions.
2. Melt 2 tablespoons of the butter and the oil over moderate heat in a medium-size skillet. Add walnuts and brown lightly. Add the tomatoes and cook, stirring often, 5 minutes or until tomatoes are tender but still hold their shape. Stir in the garlic, salt,

pepper and basil and cook 2 minutes longer. Remove from heat; cover.
3. Add broccoli to pasta during last 5 minutes cooking time. Drain.
4. Melt remaining 2 tablespoons butter in pasta kettle and return pasta and broccoli to kettle. Toss to coat with butter. Add tomato mixture, ½ cup of the broth, the cheese and parsley, and toss to blend, adding more broth if mixture seems dry.

PASTA PRIMAVERA

Makes 6 servings.

- 1 small bunch broccoli (about 1 pound)
- 2 small zucchini
- ½ pound asparagus
- 1 package (16 ounces) linguine
- 1 large clove garlic, chopped
- 1 pint cherry tomatoes, halved
- ¼ cup olive oil
- ¼ cup chopped fresh basil
  OR: 1 teaspoon leaf basil, crumbled
- ½ pound mushrooms, thinly sliced
- ½ cup frozen green peas
- ¼ cup chopped fresh parsley
- 1½ teaspoons salt
- ¼ teaspoon pepper
- ¼ teaspoon crushed red pepper
- ¼ cup (½ stick) butter
- ¾ cup heavy cream
- ⅔ cup grated Parmesan cheese

1. Wash and trim broccoli, zucchini and asparagus. Cut broccoli into bite-size pieces; cut zucchini into thin slices; cut asparagus into 1-inch pieces. Cook in boiling salted water until crisp-tender; drain; place in a large bowl.
2. Cook and drain linguine.
3. Sauté garlic and tomatoes in oil in a large skillet 2 minutes. Stir in basil and mushrooms; cook 3 minutes. Stir in peas, parsley, salt, pepper and red pepper; cook 1 minute. Add mixture to vegetables in bowl.
4. Melt butter in same skillet; stir in cream and cheese. Cook over medium heat, stirring constantly, until smooth. Add linguine; toss to coat. Stir in vegetables; heat gently.

● ● ●

Pictured opposite: (Clockwise from upper right) Pasta Primavera, page 480; Fusilli with Spinach Pesto, page 480; Spaghetti with Broccoli, Tomatoes and Walnuts, page 480; Tomato Salad Pasta, page 461.

Pastrami

PASTRAMI Highly seasoned cured beef, usually brisket, available in delicatessens or the supermarket. Originally made in eastern Europe, pastrami is dry-cured with salt and saltpeter, then the meat is rinsed, rubbed with a spice paste, smoked and cooked. It is sliced and eaten hot or cold.

PASTRY This word refers either to a baked product or a dough made of flour, butter or shortening and liquid and used for making pies, tarts, appetizers and snacks. A pastry can be sweet or savory.

Tips on Making Danish Pastry

1. It is important to keep butter enclosed in dough. If it oozes out, immediately sprinkle with flour. If dough becomes too sticky to handle, butter has probably softened. Just refrigerate 30 minutes or freeze 15 minutes before continuing.
2. Use more flour than you normally would to roll out pastries; brush off excess with soft brush before folding or filling; this way flour will not build up in pastry.
3. Since dough is very rich, it is best to let pastries rise at room temperature. Do not try to hasten the rising by using heat; doing so would melt the butter and spoil the texture.
4. If using margarine, which has a softer consistency than butter, refrigerate 20 minutes between each rolling.
5. Have ready a rolling pin, a soft pastry brush, ruler and a working surface large enough to roll dough to 30 inches.

DANISH PASTRY DOUGH

Makes enough dough for 24 individual pastries.

- **2 envelopes active dry yeast**
- **½ cup very warm water**
- **⅓ cup sugar**
- **¾ cup cold milk**
- **2 eggs**
- **4¼ cups *sifted* all-purpose flour**
- **1 teaspoon salt**
- **1 pound (4 sticks) butter or margarine**
- **Flour**

1. Sprinkle yeast into very warm water in a 1-cup measure. ("Very warm" water should feel comfortably warm when dropped on wrist.) Stir in ½ teaspoon of the sugar. Stir until yeast dissolves. Let stand undisturbed until bubbly and double in volume, about 10 minutes. Now you can tell the yeast is working.
2. Combine remaining sugar, milk, eggs, 3 cups of the flour, salt and the yeast mixture in large bowl. Beat with electric mixer at medium speed or with a wooden spoon for 3 minutes. Beat in remaining flour with spoon until dough is shiny and elastic. Dough will be soft. Scrape down side of bowl. Cover with plastic wrap. Refrigerate 30 minutes.
3. Place the sticks of butter or margarine 1 inch apart, between 2 sheets of wax paper; roll out to a 12-inch square. Chill on a cookie sheet until ready to use.
4. Sprinkle working surface heavily with flour, about ⅓ cup; turn dough out onto flour; sprinkle flour on top of dough. Roll out to an 18 × 13-inch rectangle. Brush off excess flour with a soft pastry brush.
5. Peel off top sheet of wax paper from butter; place butter, paper-side up, on one end of dough to cover two-thirds of the dough; peel off remaining sheet of wax paper. For easy folding, carefully score butter lengthwise down center, without cutting into dough. Fold uncovered third of dough over middle third; brush off excess flour; then fold remaining third of dough over middle third to enclose butter completely. Turn dough clockwise so open side is away from you.
6. *Roll out to a 24 × 12-inch rectangle using enough flour to keep dough from sticking. Fold ends in to meet on center; then fold in half to make 4 layers. Turn again so open side is away from you.
*Repeat rolling and folding this way 2 more times. Keep the dough a perfect rectangle by rolling straight up and down and from side to side. When it is necessary, chill the dough between rollings. Clean off the work-

ing surface each time and dust lightly with flour. Refrigerate dough 1 hour or more (even overnight, if you wish, to relax dough and firm up butter layers). Cut dough in half. You can see the buttery layers which, when baked, become flaky and crisp. Work with only half the dough at a time. Keep the other half refrigerated.

ALMOND CRESCENTS

Bake at 400°, then 350° for 20 to 25 minutes.
Makes 12 individual pastries.

- ½ **Danish Pastry Dough (recipe, this page)**
  Almond Filling (recipe follows)
  Slightly beaten egg
  Sugar
  Sliced almonds

1. Roll pastry on floured surface to two 20 × 15-inch rectangles; trim edges even; with a sharp knife, cut into 12 five-inch squares. Spoon filling onto one corner of each square, dividing evenly. Roll each square around filling to opposite corner. Place, point down, 2 inches apart on cookie sheet. Curve into crescent shape. Let rise in warm place until double in volume, about 30 minutes.
2. Preheat oven to 400°. Brush crescents with egg; sprinkle with sugar and almonds.
3. Place in a preheated hot oven (400°); lower heat immediately to 350°, then bake 20 to 25 minutes or until puffed and golden. Cool on wire rack.

Almond Filling: Beat ½ an 8-ounce package or can almond paste (4 ounces), ¼ cup softened butter or margarine and ¼ cup sugar in a small bowl until smooth and well blended. Makes 1 cup.

COCKSCOMBS

Bake at 400°, then 350° for 20 to 25 minutes.
Makes 12 individual pastries.

- ½ **Danish Pastry Dough (recipe, this page)**
  Almond Filling (recipe above)
  Slightly beaten egg
  Sugar

1. Roll and cut dough as in almond crescents. Spoon filling onto center of each square, dividing evenly. Spread filling slightly parallel to one edge; brush edges lightly with egg, then fold opposite edge over; press edges together to seal. Make 4 or 5 slits in sealed edge; place on cookie sheet, curving pastries slightly to resemble a cockscomb. Let rise in a warm place until double in bulk, about 30 minutes.

2. Preheat oven to 400°. Brush cockscombs with egg; sprinkle generously with sugar.

3. Place in a preheated hot oven (400°); lower heat immediately to 350°. Bake 20 to 25 minutes or until puffed and golden brown. Remove to wire rack; cool.

PRUNE DANISH

Bake at 400°, then 350° for 20 minutes.
Makes 12 individual pastries.

- ½ **Danish Pastry Dough** *(recipe page 482)*
- 1 **can (12 ounces) prune filling***
  OR: **1 jar (8 ounces) lekvar**
  Slightly beaten egg
- ½ **cup corn syrup**

1. Roll dough and cut into squares as in Almond Crescents. Spoon a rounded tablespoon prune filling onto center of each square; bring 2 opposite corners over filling to overlap about 1 inch. Place on cookie sheet 2 inches apart; let rise in a warm place until double in bulk, about 30 minutes.

2. Preheat oven to 400°. Brush pastries with beaten egg.

3. Place in a preheated hot oven (400°); lower heat to 350° immediately, then bake 20 minutes. Warm corn syrup slightly in a small saucepan; brush over pastries; bake 5 minutes longer. Remove to wire rack; cool.

Or you may use canned cherry or apple pie filling, or apricot preserves.

APRICOT BOW TIES

Bake at 400°, then 350° for 20 minutes.
Makes 12 individual pastries.

- ½ **Danish Pastry Dough** *(recipe page 482)*
- ¼ **cup apricot preserves**

Slightly beaten egg
2 **tablespoons chopped walnuts mixed with 2 tablespoons sugar**

1. Roll and cut dough as in Almond Crescents. Place 1 teaspoon of the apricot preserves along one of the edges of the pastry ½ inch in from edge. Fold over opposite edge; press edges together to seal. With a sharp knife, make a lengthwise slit in folded pastry to within 1 inch of each end. Slip one end under and pull it through the slit. Place 2 inches apart on cookie sheets. Let rise in a warm place until double in bulk, 30 to 45 minutes.

2. Preheat oven to 400°. Brush pastries with egg; sprinkle on walnuts.

3. Place in a preheated hot oven (400°); lower heat immediately to 350°. Bake 20 minutes or until golden brown. Remove to wire rack; cool.

TUNA TURNOVERS WITH MUSHROOM CHEESE SAUCE

Bake at 400° for 20 minutes.
Makes 8 turnovers.

- 1 **medium-size onion, finely chopped (½ cup)**
- 2 **tablespoons butter**
- 1 **can (9¼ ounces) tuna, drained**
- 1 **egg yolk, lightly beaten**
- 1 **can (3 to 4 ounces) chopped mushrooms, drained**
- ¼ **cup chopped pimiento-stuffed olives**
- 2½ **ounces Swiss cheese, shredded (½ cup)**
- ¼ **teaspoon salt**
- ⅛ **teaspoon pepper**
- 1 **package (17¼ ounces) pre-rolled frozen puff pastry**
- 1 **egg white, lightly beaten Mushroom Cheese Sauce (recipe follows)**
- ¼ **cup sliced pimiento-stuffed olives**

1. Sauté onion in butter in a small skillet until tender, about 3 minutes. Cool to room temperature. Flake tuna into a medium-size bowl. Stir in onion, egg yolk, mushrooms, chopped olives, cheese, salt and pepper. Blend mixture well. Refrigerate until cold.

2. Thaw frozen pastry sheets 20 min-utes at room temperature or until pliable, but still very cold. Roll out each sheet on a lightly floured surface to a 13-inch square; divide into 4 equal quarters; repeat with second sheet.

3. Divide filling equally among the 8 pastry squares, leaving a 1-inch border of uncovered pastry on all sides. Brush borders generously with some of the beaten egg white. Fold squares diagonally in half to form triangles. Press edges firmly together, then press with tines of fork to seal securely. Brush tops with egg white. Pierce each top in center with small paring knife to allow steam to escape. Arrange pies 1 inch apart on cookie sheets. Place in freezer while oven heats. Preheat oven to 450°.

4. Immediately lower temperature to hot (400°). Bake turnovers for 20 minutes.

5. Spoon Mushroom Cheese Sauce over each; garnish with olives.

Mushroom Cheese Sauce: Combine 1 can condensed cream of mushroom soup, ½ cup shredded Swiss cheese, 2 dashes liquid hot pepper seasoning and ¼ cup dry white wine in a medium-size saucepan. Cook, stirring, until cheese melts.

FRUIT TURNOVERS

Bake at 400° for 30 minutes.
Makes 8 turnovers.

- 1 **can (8¼ ounces) crushed pineapple, drained**
- 1 **can (11 ounces) mandarin oranges, drained**
- 1½ **teaspoons cornstarch**
- ⅛ **teaspoon ground cinnamon**
- 1 **package (17¼ ounces) pre-rolled frozen puff pastry**
- 1 **egg white, lightly beaten**

1. Combine pineapple, oranges, cornstarch and cinnamon in a small saucepan; heat to boiling, stirring constantly. Cool.

2. Follow steps 2 and 3 of Tuna Turnovers (above) for preparing pastry, dividing fruit mixture evenly among pastry squares.

3. Immediately lower temperature to hot (400°). Bake turnovers for 30 minutes.

•••

Pâté

PÂTÉ A well-seasoned mixture of finely minced or ground meat and/or liver, originally baked in a pastry crust. The word pâté can also be a glorified meat loaf, a savory mousse or a cocktail spread. A pâté baked in a deep oval dish is called a terrine. Pork, veal, chicken, duck, rabbit or other game, fish and even vegetables can be used to make pâtés. *Pâté de foie gras* is made of goose livers and truffles.

ELEGANT PÂTÉ

Makes about 2 cups.

- 1½ **pounds chicken livers**
- ½ **small onion**
- 1 **cup (2 sticks) butter or margarine, softened**
- ⅓ **cup minced onion**
- 1 **teaspoon salt**
  Dash cayenne
- 1 **tablespoon dry mustard**
- ¼ **teaspoon ground nutmeg**
- ⅛ **teaspoon ground cloves**

1. Cook livers with the onion half in boiling salted water to cover until tender, about 15 minutes; drain.
2. Place chicken livers, butter, minced onion, salt, cayenne, mustard, nutmeg and cloves in container of an electric blender or food processor. Cover and whirl until smooth. Turn into a serving bowl. Cover; chill for several hours. Serve with assorted crackers.

COUNTRY PÂTÉ

This smooth, mellow pâté can be baked a day or two in advance and served cold or warmed in a slow oven.

Bake at 350° for 1½ hours.
Makes 16 servings.

- 1 **pound beef liver**
- ¾ **pound boneless pork shoulder**
- ¼ **pound pork fat back**
- 1 **large onion, quartered**
- 3 **tablespoons butter or margarine**
- ¼ **cup all-purpose flour**
- 3 **teaspoons salt**
- 1 **teaspoon ground allspice**
- ¼ **teaspoon ground cloves**
- ½ **teaspoon pepper**
- 2 **cups milk**

- 2 **eggs**
  Crisp bacon strips
  Sautéed mushrooms
  Watercress or parsley

1. Soak liver in cold water for 30 minutes; pat dry on paper toweling. Trim fat and membranes from liver. Grind liver, pork, pork fat and onion twice through the fine blade of meat grinder. Place in large bowl.
2. Melt butter or margarine in medium-size saucepan; stir in flour, salt, allspice, cloves and pepper. Gradually add milk. Cook, stirring constantly, until sauce thickens and bubbles 1 minute; cool slightly. Stir hot sauce into ground liver-meat mixture; add eggs and beat with a wooden spoon until thoroughly mixed. Turn mixture into a greased 6-cup shallow baking dish.
3. Place dish in larger pan; pour boiling water into outer pan to come halfway up the side of pâté dish.
4. Bake in a moderate oven (350°) for 1½ hours or until juices run clear when pâté is pierced with a fork or a thin-bladed knife.
5. Remove from water bath and allow to cool; when pâté is cool, drain off juices; cover and refrigerate overnight or longer. Garnish with bacon, mushrooms and watercress or parsley.

CHICKEN PÂTÉ WITH PORT WINE ASPIC

Bake at 350° for 1½ hours.
Makes 12 servings.

- 1 **chicken breast half (about 8 ounces), skinned and boned**
- ½ **cup white or tawny port wine**
- 2 **tablespoons butter or margarine**
- ¾ **pound chicken livers**
- 1 **pound ground turkey, pork or veal**
- 1 **medium-size onion, minced (½ cup)**
- 2 **teaspoons salt**
- 1 **teaspoon ground coriander**
- ½ **teaspoon leaf thyme, crumbled**
- ½ **teaspoon pepper**
- 2 **eggs**
- ¾ **cup heavy cream**

- 3 **tablespoons pistachio nuts or almonds**
- 2 **bay leaves**
  Port Wine Aspic (recipe follows)
- 1 **whole canned pimiento**
  Parsley stems and sprigs

1. Cut chicken breast into long thin strips. Place in a small bowl; add port wine; let marinate several hours. Drain, reserving wine. Sauté chicken in butter in small skillet just until no pink remains. Remove to plate. Deglaze pan with reserved wine; cook until reduced to ¼ cup.
2. Chop chicken livers finely. Combine with ground turkey, onion, salt, coriander, thyme and pepper in a large bowl. Beat with wooden spoon until well blended. Gradually beat in eggs and cream. Stir in nuts and wine mixture from skillet.
3. Layer pâté mixture with chicken breast pieces in 1½-quart baking dish or loaf pan. Arrange bay leaves on top; cover with foil. Set dish in larger pan on oven shelf; fill pan half full with boiling water.
4. Bake in a moderate oven (350°) for 1½ hours until juices are no longer pink. Remove to wire rack. Cool, then chill overnight in refrigerator. Remove from pan.
5. Prepare Port Wine Aspic. Place pâté on rack over a platter to catch gelatin that drips down. Spoon a thin coating of aspic over pâté. Cut pimiento into flower-petal shapes. Arrange on top of pâté. Use parsley for stems and leaves. Brush or spoon several layers of aspic over decorations. Chill several hours. Chill remaining aspic in shallow bowl or pie plate; chop and spoon around pâté.

Port Wine Aspic: Pour 1 cup chicken broth through paper filter or double layer of cheesecloth in small saucepan; sprinkle 1 envelope unflavored gelatin over. Let stand 5 minutes to soften. Heat, stirring constantly, until gelatin is completely dissolved; remove from heat; stir in ½ cup white or tawny port wine. Place pan in larger pan of ice and water to speed thickening. Chill, stirring until syrupy.

———— •●● ————

PATTYPAN SQUASH Also called scallop or cymling, this summer squash is flat and mushroom-shaped with a scalloped edge around its midline. The skin is smooth, tender and green, white or cream in color. It is available during the summer and best when about 3 to 4 inches in diameter. The skin and seeds are tender and edible at that size. The flavor is similar to zucchini. One pound squash will make 2 to 3 servings. It can be cut up and boiled or fried, or left whole, hollowed out, stuffed and baked. See also **SQUASH**.

PEA The seeds grown in a pod of a pea plant. The most common variety is the green pea. The pods are tough and are not eaten. There are some varieties of peas in which the pods are eaten, such as sugar snaps and Chinese snow peas. Another type is dried and used for making split peas.

Buying and Storing: Fresh green peas in pods are available in some markets from March to November. Purchase about 3 pounds for 4 servings. When peas are shelled, 1 pound yields about 1 cup peas. About 95 percent of the green peas commercially grown are shelled and canned, or frozen.

Sugar snap peas have 2½- to 3-inch long, thick, fleshy pods, which contain mature peas. Chinese snow peas, also called *mange-tout,* which means "eat it all" in French, have crisp, flat pods, about 3 inches long, containing immature peas. These edible-pod peas are most plentiful from May to September. Allow one pound for 3 servings.

Dried whole or split peas are available in pound packages. Split peas are whole peas that are hulled so that the peas split. Dried yellow peas are grown from field peas; dried green peas are grown from green peas.

Store fresh peas in a plastic bag in the vegetable compartment of the refrigerator. Use within 5 days. Store dried peas in an airtight container at room temperature. Use within 8 months.

To Prepare: Shell fresh green peas and wash just before using. If the peas are small, they can be eaten raw in salads. With edible-pod peas, trim the tips and remove any strings. Wash and drain. They can be eaten raw in salads, on relish trays or served with dip.

Dried split peas do not have to be soaked before cooking; whole dried peas should be soaked.

To Cook: Shelled fresh green peas can be cooked in an inch of boiling water in a saucepan for about 10 minutes or until just tender. Drain and season. To microwave, place peas, about 3 cups, in a 1½-quart casserole dish with ¼ cup water. Cover. Microwave on high power for 5 minutes. Stir. Microwave 3 more minutes. Let stand 2 minutes; drain and season.

The edible-pod peas can be boiled quickly, steamed or stir-fried. They must be cooked quickly to retain their crispness and bright green color. To stir-fry, heat 2 tablespoons vegetable oil in a hot wok or large skillet. Add about 1 pound edible-pod peas; stir-fry until peas are coated with oil. Cover and cook 2 minutes or until crisp-tender. Season with salt or soy sauce.

Cook dried whole or split peas according to recipes for soup, or cook, drain and mash to serve as a vegetable. See also **BEANS** and **BLACKEYED PEAS**.

FRENCH-STYLE GREEN PEAS
Makes 6 to 8 servings.

- 4 **pounds fresh peas in pods, shelled**
  OR: **4 cups frozen peas**
- 2 **cups shredded lettuce**
- ¼ **cup sliced green onions**
- ½ **teaspoon salt**
- ⅛ **teaspoon pepper**
- ½ **cup water**
- ¼ **cup (½ stick) butter or margarine**
- 2 **tablespoons flour**

1. Combine peas, lettuce, green onions, salt, pepper, water and 3 tablespoons of the butter in a large saucepan; heat to boiling; cover. Simmer 10 minutes or until peas are tender.

2. While peas cook, blend remaining 1 tablespoon butter with flour to a paste in a cup.
3. Stir into pea mixture, a small amount at a time; continue cooking and stirring until mixture thickens and boils 1 minute. Spoon into a heated serving bowl.

PEAS PROVENÇAL
Makes 4 to 6 servings.

- 3 **pounds fresh peas in pods, shelled**
  OR: **3 cups frozen peas (from a 1½-pound bag)**
- 1 **large onion, chopped (1 cup)**
- 1 **clove garlic, minced**
- 2 **tablespoons olive or vegetable oil**
- 2 **medium-size tomatoes, peeled and chopped**
- ½ **teaspoon salt**
  Dash pepper

1. Cook fresh peas in boiling salted water in a medium-size saucepan for 10 minutes or until tender; drain. If using frozen peas, cook following label directions; drain.
2. While peas cook, sauté onion and garlic in oil until soft in a medium-size skillet; stir in tomatoes, salt and pepper. Cook, stirring often, 20 minutes or until slightly thickened. Stir in peas.

SPLIT PEA SOUP
Makes 6 to 8 servings.

- 1 **ham bone**
- 8 **cups water**
- 1 **package (1 pound) dried split green peas**
- 4 **medium-size carrots, pared and diced**
- 1 **medium-size onion, chopped**
- 1 **bay leaf**
  Salt and pepper

1. Combine ham bone, water, split peas, carrots, onion and bay leaf in a large kettle. Bring to boiling; cover; simmer 1 hour or until peas are soft.
2. Remove ham bone; cut off bits of meat and add to soup. Taste and season with salt and pepper, if needed; remove bay leaf.

• • •

PEA BEANS See NAVY BEANS.

PEACH The peach originated in China where it is considered a symbol of long life and immortality. From there peaches were taken west to Persia where they received the botanical name *Prunus Persica* and for many years were called "Persian apples." The peach reached Europe and later the New World via the Spanish explorers.

There are hundreds of varieties of peaches produced in the United States. Except for a few, most varieties are not easily distinguishable. They may be characterized as white-fleshed or yellow-fleshed, freestone or clingstone types. The pit of a freestone peach is easily removed from the flesh. The flesh of a clingstone peach, however, is firmly attached to the pit. Nearly all of the peaches available early in the season are clingstone; late varieties are generally freestones. Clingstone peaches have firmer flesh and are used primarily for canning. Freestone peaches are generally more flavorful, though their flesh is soft. There are also some semi-freestone peaches available early in the season.

Peaches are delicious eaten as a snack, sliced over cereal, made into desserts, preserves, or pickled and served with meat. A medium-size peach contains about 40 calories and supplies vitamins A and C.

Buying and Storing: Fresh peaches are available from early May until mid-October. Select firm, unbruised fruit. Peaches that are hard and green will not ripen properly. A ripe peach will yield to gentle palm pressure and also have a slight fragrance. Keep firm, not fully ripened peaches at room temperature a day or two until ripe, then refrigerate until ready to serve. Use within a few days.

Peaches are also marketed canned in syrup as halves or slices, or sliced and frozen.

To Prepare: Peaches need only to be rinsed with cold water and dried. If you wish, they can be peeled by dropping them into boiling water for about 30 seconds, then into cold water; the skins will slip right off. To keep peaches from darkening when cut or peeled, dip into an ascorbic acid mixture or a citrus juice.

Peach Math
1 pound peaches = 3 medium-size or 2 large
1 pound peaches = 3 cups sliced or 2½ cups diced

SPICED PEACHES
Makes 8 servings.

- 2 cans (29 ounces each) cling peach halves
- 1⅓ cups sugar
- 1 cup cider vinegar
- 4 3-inch pieces stick cinnamon
- 2 teaspoons whole cloves

1. Drain syrup from peaches into a large saucepan. Put peach halves in a large bowl.
2. Add sugar, vinegar, cinnamon and cloves to peach syrup. Bring to boiling; lower heat; simmer gently 10 minutes.
3. Pour hot syrup over peach halves; cover and cool thoroughly. Refrigerate several hours or overnight. (This is not a preserve; it will keep in refrigerator about 1 week.)

FRESH PEACH PIE
Bake at 425° for 15 minutes, then at 350° for 35 minutes.
Makes one 9-inch pie.

- ½ cup sugar
- 3 tablespoons flour
- ½ teaspoon ground cinnamon
- ¼ teaspoon salt
- 6 large ripe peaches (about 2½ pounds)
- 1 tablespoon lemon juice
- ¼ teaspoon almond extract
- 1 package piecrust mix
  Milk or water
  Sugar

1. Combine sugar, flour, cinnamon and salt in a small bowl.
2. Drop peaches into boiling water for 30 seconds; drain. Rinse with cold water. Peel, halve, pit and slice into a large bowl. Sprinkle with lemon juice and almond extract; toss to coat. Add sugar mixture; mix gently.
3. Preheat oven to 425°. Prepare piecrust mix following label directions. Roll out ⅔ to a 12-inch round on a lightly floured surface; fit into a 9-inch pie plate. Trim edge to a 1-inch overhang. Spoon in filling.
4. Roll out remaining pastry to an 11-inch round; cut into 10 strips. Weave strips over top of pie, pressing strips firmly to bottom crust. Turn edges under, flush with rim; press to make a stand-up edge; flute. Brush with milk or water; sprinkle on sugar.
5. Bake in a preheated hot oven (425°) for 15 minutes. Lower heat to moderate (350°); bake 35 minutes longer or until pastry is golden brown and juices are bubbly. Cool.

PEACH BROWN BETTY
Bake at 375° for 30 minutes.
Makes 4 servings.

- 8 slices whole wheat bread
- ¼ cup (½ stick) butter or margarine
- 1 can (29 ounces) cling peach slices
- ½ teaspoon vanilla
- ¼ teaspoon ground cinnamon
- ¼ teaspoon salt
- ⅛ teaspoon almond extract
- ½ teaspoon grated lemon rind
- 2 tablespoons lemon juice
- 1 tablespoon sugar

1. Place bread slices on a cookie sheet. Toast in a moderate oven (350°) for 20 minutes to dry out; cool. Crush into crumbs with rolling pin or whirl in blender. Melt butter in a small saucepan; stir in crumbs.
2. Drain syrup from peaches into a small saucepan. Simmer until syrup has reduced to about ½ cup.
3. Combine peaches, vanilla, cinnamon, salt, almond extract, lemon rind and juice with the ½ cup syrup.
4. Spread ⅓ of the buttered crumbs in a buttered 1-quart baking dish. Spoon in half the peach mixture. Repeat with crumbs and remaining peach mixture, topping with remaining crumbs. Sprinkle crumbs with sugar. Cover with foil.
5. Bake in a moderate oven (375°) for 15 minutes. Uncover; bake 15 minutes longer or until top is browned.

Pictured opposite: Country Pâté, page 484

Peach

PEACH-PEAR COMPOTE

When you have more peaches on hand than you planned, here's a great solution. This compote keeps well for three to four days in the refrigerator.

Makes 9 servings.

- 6 large peaches
- 3 large ripe pears
- 4 cups water
- 1 cup sugar
- 1 lemon, thinly sliced

1. Dip peaches into boiling water 30 seconds, then into ice water 1 minute. Peel, halve and pit, reserving pits. Peel and halve pears; remove core.
2. Heat water, sugar, lemon slices and reserved pits to boiling in large saucepan; lower heat. Keep syrup at a steady simmer. Add fruit, about half at a time; cook until soft on the outside but firm in center, about 10 minutes. Remove fruit to large bowl with slotted spoon as it cooks.
3. Remove pits from syrup. Pour syrup over fruit. Refrigerate until cold.

———————— •●• ————————

PEANUT BUTTER A thick paste made from shelled, roasted, blanched peanuts which are ground. Peanut butter was created in 1890 by a doctor as a nutritious, easily digested high-protein food for his patients. By law, peanut butter must be 90 percent peanuts. Commercially made peanut butter is made from roasted peanuts with salt, sweetener and emulsifiers added. Some processors make old-fashioned peanut butter from ground roasted peanuts and salt with no added ingredients. Both types of peanut butter are made in creamy and chunky styles. Peanut butter can easily be made at home using a special electric machine, an electric blender or food processor.

Store an unopened jar of peanut butter at cool, room temperature. If opened, use within 3 months. Refrigerate for longer storage.

Peanut butter is also commercially sweetened and made into peanut butter chips. They can be used in many baked recipes, in candies and sauces.

PORK SATÉ

Makes 4 servings.

- ¼ cup peanut butter
- ¼ cup grated onion
- 1 clove garlic, minced
- 1½ teaspoons light brown sugar
- ¾ teaspoon ground coriander
- ½ teaspoon ground cumin
- ⅛ teaspoon cayenne
- 2 tablespoons water
- 1 tablespoon soy sauce
- 1 tablespoon lemon juice
- 1 pound boneless pork, cut into ¾-inch cubes

1. Line the broiler pan with a sheet of aluminum foil.
2. Combine peanut butter, onion, garlic, sugar, coriander, cumin, cayenne, water, soy and lemon juice in a medium-size bowl; add pork cubes and toss to coat. Place in a single layer on prepared pan.
3. Broil 4 inches from heat for 5 minutes; turn with large cooking spoon; broil 5 minutes longer or until done. *Note:* Pork cubes can be placed on skewers and broiled. If you wish, pork can be marinated overnight in peanut butter mixture in the refrigerator.

PEANUT BUTTER AND CHOCOLATE LAYERED FUDGE

Makes about 2 pounds.

- 1 package (8 ounces) semisweet chocolate squares
- 1 can (14 ounces) sweetened condensed milk (not evaporated)
- ½ cup coarsely chopped peanuts (dry roasted or cocktail peanuts)
- 1 cup peanut butter chips (½ of a 12-ounce bag)
- 1 teaspoon butter

1. Melt 7 squares of the chocolate with half of the sweetened condensed milk (about ⅔ cup) over low heat in small saucepan; stir in peanuts. Quickly spread on bottom of wax paper-lined 8-inch square pan.
2. Melt peanut butter chips with remaining sweetened condensed milk over low heat in another small saucepan; spread over chocolate mixture.

3. Melt remaining 1 square of chocolate with the butter and quickly drizzle over the peanut butter layer with spoon or wax paper cone. Chill 2 hours or until firm. Turn out onto cutting board; peel off wax paper. Cut into squares. Store tightly covered in refrigerator for up to 3 weeks.

PEANUT BUTTER COOKIES

Bake at 375° for 12 minutes.
Makes about 5 dozen.

- 2 cups *sifted* all-purpose flour
- ¾ teaspoon baking soda
- ½ teaspoon baking powder
- ¼ teaspoon salt
- ½ cup vegetable shortening
- ½ cup peanut butter
- ½ cup firmly packed brown sugar
- ½ cup granulated sugar
- 1 egg
- ¼ cup orange juice

1. Sift flour, baking soda, baking powder and salt onto wax paper.
2. Beat shortening and peanut butter with brown and granulated sugars in a large bowl until fluffy; beat in egg. Stir in flour mixture alternately with orange juice, blending well to make a stiff dough. Chill until firm enough to handle.
3. Preheat oven to 375°. Shape dough, a teaspoonful at a time, into balls. Place 3 inches apart on ungreased cookie sheets; flatten, criss-cross fashion, with a fork.
4. Bake in a preheated moderate oven (375°) for 12 minutes or until golden. Remove from cookie sheets; cool completely on wire racks.

———————— •●• ————————

PEANUTS Botanically, peanuts are the seeds of a pea plant which mature in underground pods or shells. Peanuts are also known as goobers and ground nuts. Peanuts, which are native to South America, were grown in what is now Virginia before settlers came to America. Peanuts are commercially grown in southern states.

The two most familiar types of peanuts are Virginia and Spanish. Virginia peanuts are oval in shape; Spanish peanuts are small and round. Peanuts are available in the shell, unroasted (raw) or roasted. They can also be shelled, raw, roasted, dry-roasted and salted or unsalted. Peanuts are used commercially to make peanut oil and peanut butter.

Peanut Nutrition: An ounce of unsalted, dry-roasted peanuts contains 7 grams of protein and 160 calories. Peanuts contain niacin and no cholesterol.

Peanut Math
1 pound peanuts in shells = 2 to 2½ cups kernels
1 pound shelled peanuts = 3 cups kernels

PEAR There are literally thousands of pear varieties but only a handful are commercially grown and marketed.

Pears are harvested green because they develop a better flavor as the sugar content increases due to the conversion of starch to sugar. Pears used for cooking or baking should be firm and slightly under-ripe. Pears to be used fresh, eaten out of hand, in salads and desserts should be fully ripe. If pears are hard, let them ripen at room temperature until the fruit feels soft. Some green pears, such as the Bartlett, will turn yellow when ripe but others do not change color upon ripening.

Buying: Pears are available year-round because there are so many different varieties. Most pears are grown in California, Oregon and Washington.

Here are the major pear varieties:
Bartlett: Known as the summer pear, this variety is named for Enoch Bartlett, the owner of the property that this variety was grown on in 1817. Over two-thirds of the pears harvested in this country are Bartlett. They are available from mid-July to October. The fruit is bell-shaped; the skin is fairly thin and clear yellow when ripe. The flesh is white, smooth and juicy. Bartlett is the only variety of pears commercially canned. Canned pears are available in halves or slices,

packed in syrup, water or juice.
Anjou: A green, round, heart-shaped pear available from October to May. It is medium to large in size with a short neck. The flesh is yellowish-white, fine-textured, juicy and sweet. The color is not an indication of ripeness because this variety does not change color. When ripe, it yields to gentle pressure at the stem end.
Bosc: This variety has a long, tapering neck, a russet-brown skin and crunchy, sweet, white flesh. The fruit is medium or large in size. This pear is ideal for eating and baking. Available from September to March.
Comice: A medium to large fruit, almost round in shape, comice pears are famous as a holiday gift fruit. The skin is yellow-green, often with a red blush. The flesh is very fine, extremely juicy and not gritty. It is marketed from October to March.
Seckel: A late summer pear, small, sweet and ideal for fresh eating, canning and pickling. It has a yellow-brown skin; available from September to December.
Winter Nelis: A medium to small-size pear with a yellow-green skin. The flesh is sweet and firm, good for cooking and canning. Available from February to May.
Red Bartlett: Similar to Bartlett, differing only in skin color. The skin is bright crimson.
Forelle: A golden yellow pear with a bright red blush and red freckles. Available from December to February.
Apple-pear: A small fruit shaped like a pear with a brownish-yellow skin; the flesh is crisp and white like an apple. It looks somewhat like a small Anjou or Comice. This variety was introduced by Chinese gold miners in the California Gold Rush days. The Chinese call them Sha-li. They are also known as Japanese pears, Chalea or pear-apples. Apple-pears are available in gourmet or specialty markets from October to February.

Pear Nutrition: Pears have a fair amount of vitamin C, some A and B vitamins. A medium-size Bartlett pear has about 100 calories.

Pear Math
1 pound pears = 3 medium or 2 large
1 pound pears = 2 cups sliced or 1½ to 2 cups diced
1 can (16 ounces) slices = 1 cup drained fruit

CARAMEL CUSTARD PEAR PIE

Bake at 400° for 45 minutes.
Makes one 9-inch pie.

- ½ **package piecrust mix**
- 4 **pears (about 2 pounds)**
- 1 **tablespoon lemon juice**
- 1 **tablespoon coarsely shredded lemon rind**
- 2 **teaspoons finely chopped preserved ginger (in syrup)**
- ½ **cup firmly packed light brown sugar**
- 2 **eggs**
- 1 **cup light cream or half-and-half**
- ¼ **cup granulated sugar**

1. Prepare piecrust mix following label directions. Roll out on lightly floured surface to a 12-inch round; fit into a 9-inch pie plate. Turn edge under; pinch to make stand-up edge; flute or make rope edge.
2. Preheat oven to 400°. Peel pears, quarter, core and cut into eighths. Toss pear pieces with lemon juice in large bowl. Arrange, petal fashion, starting at outside edge, in 2 circles in bottom of pie shell. Sprinkle lemon rind, ginger and brown sugar evenly over pears; cover loosely with foil.
3. Bake in a preheated hot oven (400°) for 30 minutes.
4. Beat eggs slightly in small bowl; beat in cream; pour over pears.
5. Continue baking 15 minutes or until custard is almost set in center. Cool on wire rack 2 hours before serving.
6. Shortly before serving, melt granulated sugar in small heavy skillet; continue heating until mixture is light brown; cool slightly. Drizzle from the tip of a spoon in a back-and-forth motion over pie. If you wish to make the "spun-sugar" top, let the last tablespoon of syrup cool until syrupy thick; wave the spoon in a circular motion over center of pie to "spin" sugar in threads. If syrup hardens, place over low heat.

PEAR-CHOCOLATE-CHEESE TART

Bake at 400° for 30 minutes.
Makes one 9-inch square tart.

- ¼ cup (½ stick) butter or margarine
- ⅔ cup granulated sugar
- 1 cup *sifted* all-purpose flour
- ¼ teaspoon vanilla
- ⅔ cup ground, shelled Brazil nuts
- 1 package (12 ounces) semisweet chocolate pieces
- 2 cups heavy cream (1 pint)
- 2 packages (8 ounces each) cream cheese, softened
- 2 teaspoons vanilla
- 2 tablespoons 10X (confectioners') sugar
- 1 can (29 ounces) pear halves, drained

1. Line a 9×9×2-inch baking pan with 2 strips of aluminum foil cut to fit bottom and sides of pan; place at right angles to each other in pan to overlap in bottom.
2. Beat butter and ⅓ cup of the granulated sugar in a small bowl with electric mixer at medium speed until fluffy. Gradually beat in flour and vanilla. With spoon, stir in nuts. Press mixture into bottom and 1 inch up sides of pan with floured hands. Chill 15 minutes or until firm. Preheat oven to 400°.
3. Line crust with wax paper; fill with raw beans or rice.
4. Bake in a preheated hot oven (400°) for 25 minutes or until golden. Remove paper with beans or rice. Bake 5 minutes more; cool completely on wire rack.
5. Meanwhile, heat chocolate and cream in a medium-size saucepan over low heat until mixture comes to boiling and has consistency of heavy cream. Cool to room temperature or consistency of pudding. (If chocolate is too cold, it will solidify.)
6. Beat cream cheese, remaining ⅓ cup granulated sugar and vanilla in a large bowl with electric mixer at medium-high speed until fluffy. Remove 2 tablespoons of cooled chocolate mixture to a small bowl; stir in the 10X sugar; reserve for topping. Gradually beat remaining chocolate mixture into cheese mixture. Continue to beat until light, fluffy and almost double in volume. Lift crust from pan using foil; slide onto serving plate; discard foil. Pour chocolate mixture into shell. Chill while cutting pears.
7. Pat pears dry with paper toweling. Slice 6 halves crosswise. Arrange 1 pear in original shape in each corner of tart. Split remaining 2 halves lengthwise and place a quartered pear in between each half. Place any other pear halves in center.
8. Drizzle pears with reserved topping. (If topping is too thick to drizzle, heat until spoonable.) Garnish center of tart with Brazil nut curls and maraschino cherries, if you wish.

PEARS IN WHITE WINE

A lovely, make-ahead dessert, pears are cooked in white wine, chilled and served with fruit sauce.
Makes 8 servings.

- 8 firm, ripe pears (Bartlett or Anjou)
- 2 tablespoons lemon juice
- 3 cups dry white wine
- 1½ cups sugar
  Angelica *(optional)*
  Sauce Cardinale
- *(recipe follows)*

1. Wash pears; pare and core from blossom end but leave stems intact. Brush with lemon juice.
2. Combine wine and sugar in large saucepan; bring to boiling, stirring until sugar dissolves. Lower heat; add pears; cover. Simmer 10 minutes or until tender but still firm. Let pears cool in syrup. Refrigerate several hours or overnight.
3. Drain pears; arrange on serving dish; garnish with angelica, if you wish. Serve with Sauce Cardinale.

SAUCE CARDINALE

Makes 1½ cups.

- 1 package (10 ounces) frozen raspberries, thawed
- 1 teaspoon cornstarch
- 1 cup strawberries, fresh or frozen
- ¼ cup red currant jelly

Drain raspberries, reserving juice. Dissolve cornstarch in a little raspberry juice in a small saucepan; add remaining juice and strawberries, raspberries and jelly. Cook, stirring constantly, until mixture thickens slightly and clears. Force mixture through a sieve to remove seeds. Chill.

COPENHAGEN PEAR SALAD

Makes 4 servings.

- 1 head Boston lettuce
- 1 can (29 ounces) pear halves, drained
- ½ cup bottled blue cheese dressing
- 1 teaspoon grated orange rind

1. Line individual salad bowls with lettuce leaves; break remainder into bite-size pieces. Place 2 pear halves on top of each bed of lettuce.
2. Mix salad dressing with orange rind in a small bowl. Spoon a tablespoon over each salad. Pass the remainder.

—— ●●● ——

PECANS A nut native to the United States, pecans are related to walnuts and hickory nuts. Pecans are commercially grown in many southern states.

Pecans grow in clusters on large trees. When a nut is ripe, the green husk splits open revealing the shell of the nut. A pecan has a smooth, thin, tan shell. Pecans are available unshelled or shelled. When selecting shelled pecans, look for plump kernels that are fairly uniform in color and size. Buy halves for garnishes and pecan pieces for recipes. The pieces cost less and will save chopping time.

Store unshelled pecans in a cool, dry place and use within 6 months. Shelled pecans are best kept under refrigeration in an airtight container; use within 9 months or freeze up to 2 years.

Pecan Nutrition: Pecans are a good source of protein and vitamin A. They are rich in potassium and phosphorus. One ounce pecans contains

Pecans

about 196 calories and 3 grams of protein.

Pecan Math
1 pound in shells = 2¼ cups shelled kernels
1 pound shelled = 4 cups kernels

PECAN COOKIES

Buttery, melt-in-the-mouth confections that can be frozen.

Bake at 300° for 25 minutes.
Makes about 4 dozen.

- 1 cup (2 sticks) unsalted butter, softened
- ¼ cup sugar
- 3 tablespoons brandy
- 3 cups *sifted* all-purpose flour
- 2 cups finely chopped pecans
  10X (confectioners') sugar

1. Beat butter, sugar and brandy in a large bowl until smooth. Stir in flour to make a soft dough. Work in pecans until well blended.
2. Preheat oven to 300°. Shape dough by level tablespoonfuls into balls. Place, 1 inch apart, on ungreased cookie sheets.
3. Bake in a preheated slow oven (300°) for 25 minutes or until bottoms are brown and tops are lightly golden. Remove from cookie sheet; roll in 10X sugar. Cool; roll in sugar again. Store in airtight container.

PECAN TART

Bake at 350° for 1 hour.
Makes one 11-inch tart.

- 1 package piecrust mix
- 4 eggs
- 1 cup sugar
  Pinch salt
- ¼ cup all-purpose flour
- 2 cups light or dark corn syrup
- 2 teaspoons vanilla
- 2 cups chopped pecans

1. Prepare piecrust mix following label directions. Roll out to a 13-inch round on a lightly floured surface; fit into an 11-inch fluted tart or quiche pan with removable bottom; trim edge even with top of pan.
2. Preheat oven to 350°. Beat eggs in a large bowl just enough to break up. Stir in sugar, salt, flour, corn syrup and vanilla until mixture is well blended. Stir in pecans. Pour into prepared shell.
3. Bake in a preheated moderate oven (350°) for 1 hour or until center is almost set. (Filling will set as it cools.) Cool on wire rack.

ORANGE SUGARED PECANS

Makes 2 dozen pecan clusters.

- 1½ cups sugar
- ¼ cup water
- 3 tablespoons thawed, frozen orange-juice concentrate
- ½ teaspoon grated orange rind
- 2 cups pecan halves

1. Combine sugar, water and orange-juice concentrate in a medium-size saucepan. Bring to boiling over medium heat, stirring constantly.
2. Boil slowly, without stirring, to 240° on a candy thermometer or until a small amount of mixture dropped into cold water forms a semi-firm ball. Remove from heat.
3. Add orange rind and pecans. Stir until syrup begins to look cloudy. Drop by teaspoonfuls into clusters on wax paper. Cool. Store in airtight container.

——————— ● ● ● ———————

PEPPER This word refers to either a popular aromatic spice or a green, red or yellow vegetable. The spice pepper is obtained from grinding the dried berries of a vine now cultivated in India, Java and other tropical and subtropical countries. Whole dried berries are called peppercorns. For more information on the spice, see **PEPPERCORN.**

The peppers eaten as a vegetable or salad ingredient are fruits of a Capsicum plant. The pepper family is quite large but it can be divided into two categories—those with mild or sweet-fleshed fruits and those with hot or pungent-fleshed fruits. For information about hot peppers, see **CHILE.**

Sweet or bell peppers are native to South America. They are green when mature but if left on the plant will turn red. Both green and red peppers are readily available and can be used interchangeably.

Some sweet peppers are long and taper to a point. This type is sometimes called frying peppers. Pimiento is a heart-shaped, fleshy red pepper which is canned extensively and used to stuff pitted Spanish-style green olives. Banana peppers are slender, thick-walled yellow peppers which turn red at maturity. Cherry peppers are 1- to 1½-inch round green fruits which also turn red at maturity.

Buying and Storing: Some varieties of peppers are available year-round but they're most plentiful from May to October. Select firm, well-shaped, glossy peppers. Allow 1 medium-size green pepper per serving. Store them in a plastic bag in the vegetable compartment of the refrigerator. Use within a week.

To Prepare and Cook: For pepper shells or cups, cut off the stem ends and remove the seeds. For cut-up peppers, cut peppers into halves and remove seeds. Rinse peppers under cold water. Cut into strips or chop. Peppers can be eaten raw in salads or cooked as a vegetable. They are delicious stuffed and baked.

TUNA PEPPERS

Makes 4 servings.

- 4 medium-size sweet green or red peppers
- 1 can (7 ounces) tuna packed in olive oil, drained and flaked
- 2 hard-cooked eggs, chopped
- ½ cup chopped fresh parsley
- ½ teaspoon leaf basil, crumbled
- ¼ teaspoon pepper
- 3 tablespoons lemon juice
- 8 thin slices mozzarella cheese

1. Wash and dry peppers; place on foil-lined broiler pan.
2. Broil 5 inches from heat for 8 minutes, turning until all sides are charred. Remove from broiler and wrap in a clean towel to steam for 1 minute. Mix tuna, eggs, parsley, basil, pepper and juice in a bowl.
3. Cut peppers in half lengthwise; remove and discard seeds. Stuff peppers with tuna mixture, mounding high. Top each with 1 slice cheese.
4. Broil 5 inches from heat for 2 minutes or until cheese melts.

Pictured opposite: Pepper and Steak Sandwich, page 494

Pepper

PEPPER AND STEAK SANDWICH

Makes 4 sandwiches.

- **4 round crusty rolls with poppy seeds**
- **¼ cup (½ stick) butter or margarine, softened**
- **½ teaspoon leaf basil, crumbled**
- **½ teaspoon leaf oregano, crumbled**
- **1 medium-size onion, thinly sliced**
- **1 small green pepper, halved, seeded and cut into julienne strips**
- **1 small red pepper, halved, seeded and cut into julienne strips**
- **¼ cup vegetable oil**
- **2 tablespoons butter or margarine**
- **4 minute or cubed steaks (about 1¼ pounds)**
- **1 tablespoon red wine vinegar Salt and Pepper**

1. Cut rolls in half. Combine softened butter with basil and oregano. Spread on each cut half of roll. Place rolls on broiler pan. Broil 4 inches from heat just until lightly browned. Remove; keep warm.

2. Sauté onion, green and red peppers in oil in a large skillet until tender, about 5 minutes. Remove with slotted spoon to platter. Keep warm.

3. Add remaining 2 tablespoons butter to skillet. Sauté steaks on both sides to desired doneness. Remove to platter; keep warm.

4. Add vinegar to pan drippings in skillet. Scrape up brown bits. Cook just until bubbly, but not evaporated. Remove from heat immediately.

5. To assemble: Place a steak on bottom half of roll; top with onion-pepper mixture. Drizzle over some pan juices. Salt and pepper to taste. Cover with top half of roll.

— ●●● —

PEPPERCORN The dried berry of a woody, climbing vine that is cracked or ground to produce pepper. This variety of pepper, *Piper nigrum*, is no relation to the plant which gives us sweet red and green peppers and the hot, red peppers. (See **PEPPERS** and **CHILE**.)

A native of the East Indies, pepper vines are now cultivated in the tropics of both eastern and western hemispheres. Green, black and white peppercorns grow on the same vine. The differences between these types is in the stage of harvesting and method of processing the berries. Green peppercorns are berries picked when unripe or green. They are processed by freeze-drying or packing in water or brine. They are available in specialty or gourmet food stores.

Black peppercorns are berries picked when orange-red in color, considered almost ripe, then dried in the sun. They become hard and turn black with a shriveled appearance. White peppercorns are produced from the fully-ripened berries. The ripe red berries are soaked in water, then removed from their outer skin or hulls. The cores are dried and are the white peppercorns. Black and white peppercorns are sold whole or ground.

White pepper is less pungent than black pepper. Use it in light-colored foods where black pepper may detract from the appearance of the dish. Green peppercorns, whether dried or canned, have a subtle, pungent flavor that complements sauces, soups, meat and fish dishes.

Pink peppercorns, also called red peppercorns and *Baies Roses de Bourbon,* are the novelty spice of the 1980's. They are not true peppercorns, but rather the dried red berries of a plant related to poison ivy. These peppercorns are imported from Reunion (formerly called Bourbon), a French island off the coast of Madagascar. The plant also grows in tropical climates all over the world, including Florida, where it is considered a common weed.

Note: The Food and Drug Administration has issued a warning against ingesting pink peppercorns, believing that they can be toxic.

Szechwan peppers, also called brown peppercorns, are not related to the true peppercorns (black, white, green). They are the dried, reddish-brown fruits with opened husks of a deciduous tree native to Japan. They are produced and used in China as well as Japan. Szechwan peppers, available in specialty food stores, resemble peppercorns but are not as peppery in taste. They impart a slight anise flavor and aroma to foods. When ground, they are used as an ingredient in five-spice powder, a Chinese seasoning.

PERSIMMON A bright orange, juicy persimmon is an autumn delicacy once enjoyed by many people when it grew wild from Connecticut to Iowa and south to Florida and Texas. Today the native American persimmon is limited to home gardens and a few orchards in Indiana. American persimmons were cherry- to plum-size fruits that did not mature until after the first frost of fall.

The persimmons found in the marketplace are Oriental varieties first introduced to our country from Japan by Commodore Perry in 1855. These varieties were noted for their large size, mild flavor and the fact that they ripened after picking.

Persimmons can be eaten out of hand or the pulp used to make steamed pudding, cookies, cakes, jam and desserts.

Buying and Storing: Persimmons are available October to January. Most are California grown and are the *Hachiya* variety. This variety is slightly pointed in shape, bright orange and the size of a peach. Another variety, called *Fuyu,* is the same color but its shape is flatter, similar to a tomato. Select firm to slightly soft fruit that is well-shaped and unblemished. A persimmon is very sour-tasting if eaten before it has properly ripened. The Hachiya variety must be fully ripe and soft before eating but the Fuyu may be eaten when ripe and firm. Persimmons will ripen if left at room temperature a few days. Refrigerate as soon as they soften.

To Prepare and Serve: Rinse fruit in cold water; dry. Place persimmon on a plate, stem-end down. Cut an ''X'' at the pointed end or top with a knife. Serve with a spoon. To obtain pulp for recipes, peel back the skin in sections. Discard any seeds, slice or dice the pulp, or puree pulp in a blender or food processor.

For an unusual frozen dessert, freeze whole persimmons; wrap in freezer wrap when frozen solid. To serve, thaw slightly and serve on a plate, as above.

PHYLLO A paper-thin pastry of flour and water used primarily in Greek and Turkish cooking for both sweet and savory dishes. It is available freshly made and sold by weight or in packages in specialty shops, or frozen in pound packages and sold in supermarkets. Sometimes phyllo is called strudel pastry leaves and used to make apple strudel. For other recipes using phyllo, see **BAKLAVA** and **APPLE.**

GREEK APPLE PASTRY

A Greek version of Viennese strudel.
Bake at 350° for 50 minutes to an hour.
Makes 10 servings.

- ½ **cup walnuts**
- ¼ **cup packaged bread crumbs**
- 2½ **pounds tart cooking apples, pared and chopped (7 to 8 cups)**
- ½ **cup raisins**
- ½ **cup sugar**
- 1 **teaspoon ground cinnamon**
- ¼ **teaspoon ground nutmeg**
- ¾ **cup (1½ sticks) butter, melted**
- ½ **of a 16-ounce package frozen phyllo or strudel pastry leaves, thawed**
- 1 **tablespoon water**
  Honeyed Apple Syrup *(recipe follows)*

1. Place walnuts on cookie sheets; toast in moderate oven (350°) for 10 minutes. Cool slightly, then whirl in container of electric blender until finely chopped. Mix with bread crumbs in small bowl.
2. Combine apples, raisins, sugar, cinnamon and nutmeg in large bowl.
3. Brush bottom of 13×9×2-inch baking pan with melted butter. Fold one phyllo leaf in half or to fit bottom of pan; place in bottom of pan; brush lightly with melted butter; sprinkle with a scant tablespoon walnut mixture. Repeat about 6 or 7 times or until half of phyllo leaves are used.
4. Spread apple mixture in pan; top with remaining phyllo leaves, brushing with butter and sprinkling nut mixture between each layer. Brush top leaf with remaining butter. Preheat oven to 400°.
5. With a very sharp knife, make cuts through top 3 or 4 layers to mark pastry, making one cut lengthwise and five across. Sprinkle with water.
6. Place in a very hot oven (400°), then turn heat to 350° and bake 50 minutes to 1 hour or until pastry is golden and apples are tender. Remove pan to wire rack; cut all the way through the markings. Pour cooled Honeyed Apple Syrup over. Cool on wire rack.

Honeyed Apple Syrup: Combine ½ cup apple juice or cider, ½ cup sugar and 3×1-inch strip of lemon rind in small saucepan. Bring to boiling; lower heat; simmer 5 minutes. Remove from heat; stir in 2 to 3 tablespoons honey; cool.

● ● ●

PICKLES Vegetables or fruits preserved by using salt and/or sugar with vinegar. Cucumbers and peaches are among the favorite pickled foods. For more information, see **CANNING.**

PICKLED MUSHROOMS

A tempting appetizer to serve.
Makes 5 cups.

- 2 **cups water**
- ¾ **cup vegetable oil**
- ½ **cup lemon juice**
- 3 **celery stalks, cut into 3-inch pieces**
- 1 **clove garlic, halved**
- ½ **teaspoon ground coriander**
- ¼ **teaspoon leaf thyme, crumbled**
- ⅛ **teaspoon fennel seeds**
- ½ **teaspoon salt**
- 8 **peppercorns**
- 1½ **pounds small mushrooms**
- 1 **jar (4 ounces) pimientos, drained and sliced**

Combine water, oil, lemon juice, celery, garlic, coriander, thyme, fennel, salt and peppercorns in a medium-size saucepan; bring to boiling. Lower heat; add mushrooms; simmer 5 minutes. Pour into a large bowl. Cool. Add pimientos. Cover; refrigerate. Will keep for up to 1 week.

DILLED ZUCCHINI PICKLES

Makes 12 half pints.

- 6 **pounds zucchini**
- 2 **cups thinly sliced celery**
- 2 **large onions, chopped (2 cups)**
- ½ **cup sugar**
- 2 **tablespoons dill seed**
- 2 **cups distilled white vinegar**
- 6 **cloves garlic, halved**

1. Pare zucchini, cut in half lengthwise, scoop out seeds and discard. Cut zucchini into thin 4-inch long strips (makes about 16 cups).
2. Combine zucchini, celery and onions in a large bowl (use 2 if necessary). Cover top of vegetables completely with ice cubes. Cover with a clean towel; let stand at room temperature for 3 hours; drain.
3. Meanwhile, wash and rinse twelve 8-ounce jars and their 2-piece lids. Keep jars immersed in kettle of hot water until you are ready to use them. Place lids in saucepan of boiling water just before using.
4. Place sugar, dill seed and vinegar in a large, heavy enamel or stainless steel kettle; bring to boiling, stirring constantly. Add zucchini and reheat to boiling, stirring frequently.
5. Pack the zucchini in drained, hot jars with a slotted spoon, using a wide-mouth funnel, filling to within ⅛-inch of the top; add half clove garlic to each jar. Pour enough boiling liquid into jars to cover zucchini, at the same time leaving ⅛-inch head space. Run a thin wooden or plastic spoon handle or other non-metallic utensil around edge of jars between food and jar to release any trapped air bubbles. Wipe jar rims and seal.
6. Process in boiling water bath for 15 minutes. Remove jars from water bath; cool; check seals; label.

Pickles

PICCALILLI

Makes 6 half pints.

- **1 pound green tomatoes (3 medium-size)**
- **1 large red pepper, seeded and chopped (¾ cup)**
- **1 large green pepper, seeded and chopped (¾ cup)**
- **1 to 2 tablespoons finely chopped hot pepper**
- **2 large onions, chopped (2 cups)**
- **1 small head cabbage, cored and chopped (6 cups)**
- **1 tablespoon salt**
- **1 cup sugar**
- **1 tablespoon mustard seeds**
- **1 tablespoon celery seeds**
- **1 cup light corn syrup**
- **2 cups cider vinegar**

1. Core tomatoes; chop coarsely (you should have 3 cups). Combine tomatoes with remaining ingredients in a large stainless steel or enamel kettle.

2. Bring mixture to boiling, stirring occasionally. Lower heat and cook about 30 minutes or until syrup is slightly thickened and vegetables are crisp-tender.

3. Ladle vegetables into 6 hot, 8-ounce jars with a slotted spoon, leaving ½-inch head space. Pour the syrup into jars, covering vegetables and leaving ¼-inch head space. Wipe rims and seal.

4. Process in boiling water bath for 10 minutes. Remove; cool; label.

PICKLED PEACHES AND PEARS

Makes 5 pints peaches and 6 pints pears.

- **12 cups sugar**
- **4 cups cider vinegar**
- **4 3-inch pieces stick cinnamon**
- **2 tablespoons whole cloves**
- **14 large peaches, peeled, halved and pitted (about 6 pounds)**
- **24 medium-size pears**
- **1 1-inch piece ginger root (optional)**

1. Combine sugar, vinegar, cinnamon and cloves in a large kettle. Bring to boiling; simmer 5 minutes.

2. Lower peach halves into kettle with a slotted spoon; bring to boiling;

lower heat; simmer 15 minutes or just until peaches are tender.

3. Remove kettle from heat; cover; let stand 12 to 18 hours at room temperature. Next day, bring mixture to boiling. Ladle into 5 hot, 16-ounce jars, leaving ½-inch head space. Seal and process in boiling water bath for 20 minutes. Remove; cool; label.

4. Pare, halve and core pears. Add dry ginger root to remaining syrup in kettle, if you wish. (You should have about 8 cups of syrup left.) Bring to boiling; lower pear halves into kettle with a slotted spoon; bring to boiling; lower heat; simmer 10 minutes or just until pears are tender.

5. Remove kettle from heat; cover; let stand 12 to 18 hours at room temperature. Next day, bring mixture to boiling. Ladle into 6 hot, 16-ounce jars, leaving ½-inch head space. Seal and process in boiling water bath for 20 minutes. Remove; cool; label.

GARDEN MUSTARD PICKLES

Makes 7 pints.

- **1 small cauliflower, separated into flowerets**
- **1 pound small white onions, peeled**
- **6 green tomatoes, cored and cut into wedges**
- **6 pickling cucumbers, cut into 1-inch pieces**
- **2 large green peppers, halved, seeded and cut into 1-inch pieces**
- **2 large red peppers, halved, seeded and cut into 1-inch pieces**
- **⅓ cup kosher or canning salt**
- **½ cup firmly packed brown sugar**
- **3 tablespoons dry mustard**
- **2 teaspoons turmeric**
- **2 teaspoons mustard seeds**
- **2 teaspoons celery seeds**
- **6 cups cider vinegar**
- **½ cup all-purpose flour**
- **1 cup cold water**

1. Combine vegetables with salt in a large glass or ceramic bowl.

2. Cover bowl with plastic wrap; let stand 12 to 18 hours at room temperature. Next day, drain vegetables; spoon into a large kettle. Add brown

sugar, mustard, turmeric, mustard and celery seeds; stir in cider vinegar.

3. Bring to boiling, stirring often; lower heat; simmer 15 minutes or until vegetables are tender. Combine flour and cold water in a small bowl to make a smooth paste. Stir slowly into bubbling liquid; cook, stirring, until mixture thickens and bubbles 3 minutes.

4. Ladle into 7 hot, 16-ounce jars, leaving ½-inch head space. Wipe rims and seal. Process in boiling water bath for 5 minutes. Remove; cool; label.

— ●●● —

PICNIC FOODS The best foods for eating outdoors at a picnic are those that can be made ahead, are easily transported and require a minimum of equipment or cooking before serving. Foods that melt, wilt or deteriorate easily should be avoided. Whether your picnic is a tailgate supper before or after a game, or an outing in the park, here are some picnic foods to take along.

LAMB AND MUSHROOM KABOBS

Cook on hibachi 12 to 15 minutes. Makes 8 servings.

- **⅓ cup catsup**
- **¼ cup lemon juice**
- **2 tablespoons soy sauce**
- **1 tablespoon leaf rosemary, crumbled**
- **½ teaspoon salt**
- **½ cup olive or vegetable oil**
- **2 pounds lean lamb, cut into 1- to 1½-inch cubes**
- **1½ pounds large mushrooms**

1. Combine catsup, lemon juice, soy sauce, rosemary, salt and oil in a small bowl; mix with fork until well blended.

2. Pour marinade over lamb cubes in large bowl; cover. Refrigerate overnight.

3. Halve or quarter mushrooms; thread onto metal skewers alternating with cubes of meat. Wrap skewers in foil; pour marinade into jar with tight-fitting lid.

4. Cook kabobs over grayed coals, turning and brushing often with marinade, 12 to 15 minutes for pink lamb.

CUCUMBER AND POTATO SOUP

Makes 4 to 6 servings.

- **1 large cucumber, pared, seeded and diced (1½ cups)**
- **¼ cup sliced green onions**
- **2 tablespoons butter or margarine**
- **2 cups milk**
- **1 can condensed cream of potato soup**
- **½ teaspoon salt**
- **⅛ teaspoon cayenne**
- **⅛ teaspoon ground nutmeg**
- **1 cup light cream or plain yogurt**

1. Sauté cucumber and onions in butter in a large saucepan until soft, about 5 minutes. Stir in milk and potato soup. Bring to boiling, stirring constantly. Lower heat; cover.
2. Simmer, stirring often, 5 minutes. Stir in salt, cayenne, nutmeg and cream or yogurt; heat through. (Do not boil if using yogurt.)
3. Puree mixture, ½ at a time, in container of electric blender or food processor. Cool, then chill several hours. When serving, taste and add additional seasoning, if needed. If chilled soup is too thick, add more milk or cream. Pour into a 2-quart insulated container for toting.

RICE AND VEGETABLE SALAD

An easy-to-carry salad that does not wilt.

Makes 8 servings.

- **1 cup uncooked brown rice**
- **1 cup chopped celery**
- **1 cup chopped green onions**
- **1 cup shredded carrots**
- **1 cup shredded zucchini**
- **1 cucumber, pared, seeded and chopped**
- **¼ cup chopped fresh parsley**
- **½ cup white wine vinegar**
- **½ cup olive or vegetable oil**
- **1½ teaspoons salt**
- **1 large tomato**
- **4 lemon slices, halved**
- **8 ripe olives**
  Parsley sprigs

1. Cook rice following label directions; cool; chill 1 hour or until cold.
2. Add celery, onions, carrots, zucchini, cucumber, parsley, vinegar, oil and salt to chilled rice; toss to mix well. Spoon salad into shallow plastic container with a snap-on cover. Cover; refrigerate.
3. To serve: Spoon into bowl. Cut tomato into 4 slices (chop the ends and add to salad); cut each slice in half; arrange on top of salad with lemon slices and olives. Garnish with parsley sprigs.

HERB-CHEESE FILLED BREAD

An unusual bread for brunch or supper.

Bake at 350° for 50 minutes.
Makes 1 nine-inch loaf.

- **1 cup milk**
- **6 tablespoons (¾ stick) butter or margarine**
- **1 tablespoon sugar**
- **2 teaspoons salt**
- **1 envelope active dry yeast**
  Pinch sugar
- **¼ cup very warm water**
- **3¼ to 3½ cups *unsifted* all-purpose flour**
- **2 eggs**
- **½ teaspoon ground coriander**
- **¼ teaspoon pepper**
- **¼ cup chopped parsley**
- **1½ pounds Muenster cheese, shredded**
- **1 tablespoon sesame seeds**

1. Combine milk, 3 tablespoons of the butter, sugar and salt in a small saucepan; heat until butter melts. Cool to lukewarm.
2. Sprinkle yeast and the pinch sugar into very warm water in a large bowl. ("Very warm water" should feel comfortably warm when dropped on wrist.) Stir until yeast dissolves. Let stand until bubbly, about 5 minutes.
3. Stir milk into yeast mixture. Gradually stir in 3 cups of the flour; turn out onto lightly floured surface. Knead until smooth and elastic, about 8 minutes, using only as much remaining flour as needed to keep dough from sticking.
4. Place dough in buttered large bowl; turn to bring buttered side up. Cover with a towel. Let rise in a warm place, away from drafts, 1 hour or until double in volume.
5. Soften remaining 3 tablespoons butter in large bowl. Beat eggs slightly in a small bowl, reserving 1 tablespoon for glaze. Add remaining eggs, coriander, pepper and parsley to butter. Stir in cheese; toss well. Grease a 9 × 1½-inch layer pan; sprinkle with half of the sesame seeds.
6. Punch dough down; turn out onto very lightly floured surface; roll or stretch to a 16-inch round. Center dough over prepared pan; fill with cheese mixture. Gather edges of dough up and over filling into center, pleating the dough into large folds; hold the ends of the dough that meet in center between fingers; pinch together, then twist into a little knob.
7. Let rise again in a warm place, away from drafts, 45 minutes or until almost double in volume. Preheat oven to 350°. Brush bread with reserved egg. Sprinkle with remaining seeds.
8. Bake in a preheated moderate oven (350°) for 50 minutes or until loaf is golden and sounds hollow when tapped. Remove from pan to wire rack to cool. Serve slightly warm or at room temperature.

SALAD BOWL SANDWICH

Makes 6 servings.

- **1 can (7 ounces) tuna, drained and flaked**
- **1 cup cherry tomatoes, halved**
- **1 medium-size green pepper, halved, seeded and diced**
- **¼ cup diced red onion**
- **½ cup sliced pitted ripe olives**
- **1 package (8 ounces) mozzarella cheese, diced**
- **½ cup bottled oil and vinegar salad dressing**
- **2 teaspoons leaf basil, crumbled**
- **6 whole wheat or white pita breads**

1. Combine tuna, cherry tomatoes, green pepper, red onion, olives, mozzarella cheese, oil and vinegar dressing and basil in a large bowl; toss to mix.
2. Turn into an insulated bowl with tight-fitting cover for toting.
3. To serve: Open pocket of each pita bread with a small knife; tuck tuna filling into pita bread pockets.

COUNTRY MEAT LOAF

Bake at 350° for 1 hour in loaf pan or 45 minutes in ring mold.
Makes 6 to 8 servings.

- **2 pounds ground chuck**
- **1 large onion, finely chopped (1 cup)**
- **½ cup packaged bread crumbs**
- **2 eggs**
- **½ cup dairy sour cream**
- **2 tablespoons catsup**
- **1 tablespoon Dijon mustard**
- **¼ cup chopped fresh parsley**
- **1½ teaspoons salt**
- **½ teaspoon pepper**

1. Combine chuck, onion, bread crumbs, eggs, sour cream, catsup, mustard, parsley, salt and pepper in a large bowl; mix well.
2. Spoon mixture into a lightly greased 9×5×3-inch loaf pan or a 6½-cup ring mold. Spread evenly and press down firmly.
3. Bake in a moderate oven (350°) for 1 hour for the loaf pan or 45 minutes for ring mold or until meat loaf shrinks from sides. Remove from oven; pour off any juices. Unmold onto serving platter; cool. Wrap with plastic wrap and refrigerate until ready to tote. Wrap meat loaf with foil for toting.

JUMBO DOUBLE CHOCOLATE CHIP COOKIES

A fun variation of a popular cookie.
Bake at 375° for 12 minutes.
Makes 1½ dozen 4- to 5-inch cookies.

- **1 recipe Chocolate Chip Cookies (recipe follows)**
- **1 recipe Double Chocolate Chip Cookies (recipe follows)**

1. Preheat oven to 375°. For each cookie, drop a rounded tablespoonful of each dough side by side on a greased cookie sheet. Spread each dough to form a 3-inch semicircle joined to form a large two-toned cookie. Space cookies 5 to 6 inches apart.
2. Bake in a preheated moderate oven (375°) for 12 minutes or until golden brown. Remove from cookie sheet to wire rack with wide spatula. Cool completely.

CHOCOLATE CHIP COOKIES

Bake at 375° for 12 minutes.
Makes 1½ dozen.

- **½ cup *unsifted* all-purpose flour**
- **½ teaspoon baking soda**
- **½ cup whole wheat flour**
- **½ cup (1 stick) butter or margarine, softened**
- **¾ cup sugar**
- **1 egg**
- **1 teaspoon vanilla**
- **1 package (6 ounces) semisweet chocolate pieces**
- **½ cup chopped nuts**

1. Sift flour and baking soda onto wax paper. Add whole wheat flour.
2. Preheat oven to 375°. Beat butter, sugar, egg and vanilla in a medium-size bowl until fluffy.
3. Gradually stir in flour mixture until well blended. Stir in chocolate pieces and nuts.
4. Drop by slightly rounded table-spoonfuls onto lightly greased cookie sheets.
5. Bake in a preheated moderate oven (375°) for 12 minutes or until golden brown. Remove from cookie sheets to wire racks; cool completely.

DOUBLE CHOCOLATE CHIP COOKIES

Bake at 375° for 12 minutes.
Makes 1½ dozen.

- **½ cup *unsifted* all-purpose flour**
- **½ teaspoon baking soda**
- **½ cup whole wheat flour**
- **½ cup (1 stick) butter or margarine, softened**
- **¾ cup sugar**
- **1 egg**
- **2 squares unsweetened chocolate, melted**
- **1 teaspoon vanilla**
- **1 package (6 ounces) semisweet chocolate pieces**
- **½ cup chopped walnuts *(optional)***

1. Sift flour and baking soda onto wax paper. Mix in whole wheat flour.
2. Preheat oven to 375°. Beat butter, sugar, egg, chocolate and vanilla in a large bowl until fluffy.
3. Stir in flour mixture, chocolate pieces and nuts until blended.
4. Drop by slightly rounded table-spoonfuls onto greased cookie sheets.
5. Bake in a preheated moderate oven (375°) for 12 minutes or until cookies feel firm. Remove to wire racks; cool completely.

● ● ●

PIE A dish of meat, fish, poultry or fruit covered with a crust and baked. The crust is usually a pastry but a pie can be covered with biscuits, mashed potatoes, crumbs or meringue. Here are recipes for main-dish and dessert pies.

MAIN-DISH PIES

HAMBURGER-VEGETABLE PIE

Bake at 450° for 15 minutes.
Makes 6 servings.

- **1 medium-size onion, chopped (½ cup)**
- **1 to 2 cloves garlic, minced**
- **1 tablespoon vegetable oil**
- **1½ pounds lean ground beef**
- **1 can (16 ounces) tomatoes**
- **1 can (6 ounces) tomato paste**
- **2 teaspoons salt**
- **¼ teaspoon pepper**
- **1 teaspoon dried parsley flakes**
- **½ teaspoon leaf rosemary, crumbled**
- **1 can (16 ounces) whole-kernel corn, drained**
- **1 package (10 ounces) frozen green peas**
- **2 packages (4.5 ounces each) refrigerated buttermilk biscuits**

1. Sauté onion and garlic in oil in a large skillet until tender, about 5 minutes. Add beef and cook, stirring occasionally with fork, until brown. Drain off excess fat. Add tomatoes, tomato paste, salt, pepper, parsley flakes and rosemary. Bring to boiling; lower heat; simmer 15 minutes.
2. Preheat oven to 450°. Remove skillet from heat. Stir in corn and peas; heat thoroughly. Spoon into a 3-quart shallow baking dish. Arrange refrigerated biscuits over top.
3. Bake in a preheated very hot oven (450°) for 15 minutes or until biscuits are golden brown. Let stand 10 minutes before serving.

Pictured opposite: Rice and Vegetable Salad, page 497; Herb-Cheese Filled Bread, page 497; Lamb and Mushroom Kabobs, page 496; Jumbo Double Chocolate Chip Cookies, page 499; Cucumber and Potato Soup, page 497

ITALIAN CHEESE AND VEGETABLE PIE

Bake at 375° for 45 minutes.
Makes 6 servings.

- 3 **tablespoons vegetable or olive oil**
- 2 **medium-size zucchini, sliced thin**
- 2 **medium-size onions, sliced thin**
- 2½ **teaspoons salt**
- 1 **clove garlic, crushed**
- 3 **tablespoons chopped fresh parsley**
- 1 **can (16 ounces) tomatoes**
- 1 **can (8 ounces) tomato sauce**
- ½ **teaspoon leaf oregano, crumbled**
  Dash pepper
- 1 **container (15 ounces) ricotta cheese**
- 4 **eggs**
- 1½ **cups milk**
- 1 **package (8 ounces) refrigerated crescent rolls**
- 4 **ounces (½ package) mozzarella cheese, sliced**

1. Heat 2 tablespoons of the oil in large skillet; add zucchini and onion. Sauté, stirring often, until tender, about 10 minutes. Stir in 1 teaspoon of the salt; remove mixture to bowl.
2. In same skillet in remaining oil, sauté garlic and parsley, stirring constantly, 1 minute; add tomatoes, tomato sauce, oregano, ½ teaspoon of the salt and the pepper. Cook, stirring occasionally and mashing the tomatoes with a spoon, 15 minutes or until reduced to 2 cups.
3. Beat ricotta cheese, eggs and remaining 1 teaspoon salt in large bowl; gradually beat in milk. Preheat oven to 375°.
4. Line a fluted 10-inch quiche dish or 10-inch pie plate with unrolled and separated crescent rolls, overlapping slightly and pressing edges of dough triangle rolls together. Spread vegetables in bottom of shell; spoon about ¼ cup tomato sauce over. Set dish on oven shelf, then pour in cheese mixture.
5. Bake in a preheated moderate oven (375°) for 40 minutes or just until set in center. Arrange cheese slices on top of pie; spoon some of the tomato sauce in between slices. Bake 5 minutes longer or until cheese is melted. Garnish with parsley, olives and rolled anchovies, if you wish. Serve in wedges with remaining tomato sauce.

TAMALE PIE

Spicy corned beef with a cornmeal crust gives this "Tex-Mex" pie a zingy combination of flavors.

Bake at 400° for 1 hour.
Makes 6 servings.

- 1½ **cups yellow cornmeal**
- ¾ **teaspoon salt**
- 1 **cup cold water**
- 3 **cups boiling water**
- 2 **tablespoons vegetable oil**
- 1 **medium-size onion, chopped (½ cup)**
- ½ **cup chopped green pepper**
- 1 **clove garlic, minced**
- 1 **can (12 ounces) corned beef*, chopped**
- 2 **cans (8 ounces each) tomato sauce**
- 2 **to 3 tablespoons chili powder**
- ½ **to ¾ teaspoon salt**
- ½ **teaspoon ground cumin**
- 4 **ounces Cheddar cheese, shredded (1 cup)**
  OR: 6 slices American cheese, cut into ¼-inch pieces
- ¾ **cup pitted ripe olives, halved**

1. Mix cornmeal, salt and cold water in a medium-size saucepan. Stir in boiling water; bring to boiling; cook over moderate heat, stirring frequently, until mixture is thick, about 3 to 5 minutes. Remove from heat. Cool.
2. Meanwhile, heat oil in large skillet; sauté onion, green pepper and garlic until golden and tender, but not brown.
3. Break up corned beef in skillet; add tomato sauce, chili powder, salt and cumin. Stir over moderate heat until mixture comes to boiling. Remove from heat; add cheese and olives; stir until cheese is melted.
4. Line the sides, but not the bottom, of a buttered, 2-quart, deep oven-proof casserole with ¾ of the corn-meal mixture using a metal spatula. (Dip spatula in cold water to make spreading easier.)
5. Spoon corned beef mixture into center of casserole; spoon remaining cornmeal around edges on top of casserole, leaving a 2- to 3-inch center. Using a wet metal spatula, spread cornmeal smoothly over top and towards edges of casserole, sealing completely.
6. Bake in a hot oven (400°) for 1 hour or until lightly browned on top and bubbling in the middle. Let stand 15 minutes before serving. Garnish with green pepper rings, if you wish.

For the corned beef, substitute 1 can (16 ounces) chili with beans and 1 can (16 ounces) red kidney beans, drained, and use only 1 can tomato sauce.

CHICKEN-MUSHROOM PIE WITH DILL CRUST

Bake at 450° for 20 minutes.
Makes 6 servings.

- 2½ **cups diced cooked chicken**
- 1 **can condensed cream of celery soup**
- 2 **jars (2½ ounces each) sliced mushrooms**
- ½ **cup sliced celery**
- ½ **cup diced green pepper**
- 1 **teaspoon bottled steak sauce**
- ½ **teaspoon leaf marjoram, crumbled**
- ½ **package piecrust mix**
- ½ **teaspoon dillweed**

1. Combine chicken, celery soup, mushrooms with liquid, celery, green pepper, steak sauce and marjoram in a large skillet. Heat slowly until bubbly hot, about 10 minutes. Turn into a 4-cup shallow baking dish.
2. Preheat oven to 450°. Prepare piecrust mix following label directions, adding dillweed. Roll out to fit top of baking dish; cover dish with pastry; turn edge under, flush with rim; flute. Cut a 6-inch "X" in center of pastry. Fold corners back.
3. Bake in a preheated very hot oven (450°) for 20 minutes or until crust is golden brown. Let stand 10 minutes before serving.

Pictured opposite: (From top) English Pub Pie, page 502; Beef and Vegetable Pie, page 502; Italian Cheese and Vegetable Pie, page 501

ENGLISH PUB PIE

Bake at 350° for 1 hour, 40 minutes.
Makes 12 servings.

- **2 whole chicken breasts (about 12 ounces each)**
- **½ pound cooked ham, diced**
- **1 can (6 ounces) chopped mushrooms**
- **½ cup chopped fresh parsley**
- **2 teaspoons salt**
  Flaky Pastry (recipe follows)
- **4 hard-cooked eggs, peeled**
- **1 egg**
- **1 tablespoon plus 1½ cups water**
- **½ teaspoon leaf tarragon, crumbled**
- **1 envelope unflavored gelatin**

1. Bone and skin chicken; dice; reserve skin and bones for step 7.
2. Mix ham and chicken in a large bowl. Fold in mushrooms and liquid, parsley and 1 teaspoon of the salt until well blended.
3. Roll out ¾ of Flaky Pastry to a 16×12-inch rectangle on a lightly floured pastry board. Fit into a 9×5×3-inch loaf pan, pressing pastry into bottom and sides of pan.
4. Spoon ⅓ of meat mixture into pan; place hard-cooked eggs down center of filling; spoon remaining filling around and on top of eggs.
5. Preheat oven to 350°. Roll out remaining pastry to a 10×6-inch rectangle on a lightly floured pastry board. Cut out two ½-inch vents near the center of pastry. Arrange pastry over filling; trim to ½ inch; turn under and flute edges to make a stand-up rim. Cut pastry trims into leaf and stem shapes. Beat egg with 1 tablespoon water in a cup; brush pastry with egg; arrange pastry trims in design. Brush again with egg wash.
6. Bake in preheated moderate oven (350°) for 1 hour and 40 minutes, brushing with egg after 1 hour, or until pastry is golden and filling bubbles through vents in pastry. Cool in pan.
7. While pie bakes, combine chicken bones and skin, 1½ cups water, remaining salt and tarragon in medium-size saucepan. Heat to boiling; cover saucepan; lower heat; simmer 45 minutes. Strain broth into a 2-cup measure; skim off fat as it rises to the surface. You should have 1 cup of broth. If not, add water. Chill.
8. After pie is baked, sprinkle gelatin over chilled broth to soften. Pour mixture into a small saucepan; heat until gelatin dissolves. Gradually pour broth through the two vents in pastry. Cool pie on wire rack 1 hour; chill overnight.

Flaky Pastry: Sift 3 cups *sifted* all-purpose flour and 1 teaspoon salt into a large bowl. Cut in 1 cup shortening with a pastry blender until mixture is crumbly. Sprinkle 6 to 8 tablespoons ice cold water over mixture, 1 tablespoon at a time; mix lightly with a fork, just until pastry holds together and leaves the side of the bowl clean. Gather into a ball. Makes enough pastry for one 9×5×3-inch pan or two-crust 10-inch pie.

BEEF AND VEGETABLE PIE

Bake at 400° for 30 minutes.
Makes 6 servings.

- **1 package piecrust mix**
- **1 large onion, chopped (1 cup)**
- **2 carrots, sliced (1 cup)**
- **2 cups chopped green cabbage**
- **2 tablespoons butter or margarine**
- **1 pound ground chuck**
- **1 cup hot water**
- **1 envelope (¾ ounce) instant brown gravy mix**
- **2 tablespoons chopped fresh parsley**
- **1 teaspoon salt**
- **½ teaspoon leaf savory, crumbled**
- **¼ teaspoon pepper**
- **1 egg, slightly beaten**

1. Prepare piecrust mix following label directions; chill 30 minutes.
2. Meanwhile, sauté onion, carrots and cabbage in hot butter or margarine in large skillet, stirring often, until tender and slightly browned, about 15 minutes. Remove to a large bowl.
3. In same skillet, sauté meat over high heat, stirring constantly, until it loses its pink color. Lower heat, stir in water; cook and stir to loosen browned bits in pan. Stir in gravy mix, parsley, salt, savory and pepper; cover, simmer 5 minutes; add to vegetables.
4. Preheat oven to 400°. Roll pastry to a 16-inch round on a lightly floured surface. Carefully slide a cookie sheet under pastry to within 1 inch from edge of cookie sheet. Spoon meat and vegetable mixture onto pastry half on cookie sheet 2 inches in from edge; fold other half over to make a half circle. Press edges together to seal firmly; turn up and crimp edges. Mix egg with 1 tablespoon water; brush over top of pie. Make a few slits in top for steam to escape.
5. Bake in a preheated hot oven (400°) for 30 minutes or until golden brown. Slide onto a cutting board; cut into slices for serving. Garnish with parsley and tomatoes, if you wish.

DESSERT PIES

MINCEMEAT-ICE CREAM PIE

Bake at 350° for 10 minutes.
Makes 8 servings.

- **1½ cups pecan halves, finely chopped (about 6 ounces)**
- **3 tablespoons sugar**
- **2 tablespoons butter, melted**
- **1 cup prepared bottled mincemeat**
- **1 quart vanilla ice cream**
- **½ teaspoon ground cinnamon**
- **½ teaspoon ground ginger**
- **¼ teaspoon ground allspice**
- **1 tablespoon grated orange rind**
- **½ pint heavy cream, whipped**

1. Combine chopped pecans, sugar and melted butter in a medium-size bowl; mix well. Press firmly and evenly onto the bottom and side of a well greased 9-inch pie plate.
2. Bake in a moderate oven (350°) for 10 minutes. Cool thoroughly.
3. Spread prepared mincemeat evenly onto the bottom of cooled prepared shell.
4. Soften ice cream in a chilled medium-size bowl; blend in cinnamon, ginger, allspice and grated rind. Spread the ice cream evenly over mincemeat layer. Freeze until firm.
5. To serve: Remove pie from freezer 20 minutes before serving. Garnish with whipped cream.

Pictured opposite: (From top) Lime Chiffon Pie, page 504; Tropical Pineapple Chiffon Pie, page 504; Peppermint Chiffon Pie, page 504

Pie

TROPICAL PINEAPPLE CHIFFON PIE

Makes one 9-inch pie.

- 20 brown-edge vanilla wafers
- ½ cup flaked coconut
- ¼ cup (½ stick) butter or margarine
- 1 envelope unflavored gelatin
- ⅓ cup sugar
- 4 eggs, separated
- 1 medium-size lemon
- 1 can (20 ounces) crushed pineapple in pineapple juice
- ½ cup heavy cream

1. Crush cookies in plastic bag with rolling pin.* (Makes 1 cup.) Heat coconut in a medium-size heavy skillet over medium heat, stirring constantly, until golden brown. Stir in butter until melted; remove from heat; stir in cookie crumbs. Press crumb mixture against side and bottom of 9-inch pie plate. Chill while preparing filling.
2. Mix gelatin and 3 tablespoons of the sugar in a medium-size heavy saucepan; add egg yolks and beat with wooden spoon until well blended. Grate rind from lemon; measure and reserve 2 teaspoons. Squeeze lemon; measure 2 tablespoons juice. Drain juice from pineapple, ½ to ¾ cup; add to gelatin mixture along with lemon juice; stir to blend in.
3. Cook gelatin mixture over low to medium heat, stirring constantly, 8 to 10 minutes or until gelatin is completely dissolved and mixture thickens slightly and coats a spoon. Cool slightly; stir in lemon rind and pineapple. (For a smoother pie, puree pineapple in container of electric blender until smooth before adding to gelatin mixture.) Place pan in a bowl of ice and water to speed setting; chill, stirring often, until mixture starts to thicken.
4. While pineapple mixture chills, beat egg whites in a medium-size bowl until foamy-white; gradually beat in remaining sugar until meringue stands in soft peaks. Beat cream in a small bowl until stiff.
5. Fold whipped cream and meringue into gelatin mixture until no streaks of white remain. Spoon into the chilled piecrust, mounding high. Chill 4 hours or until firm. Garnish with additional cream, pineapple and toasted coconut, if you wish.

Cookies may be whirled in blender but the crumbs will be much finer and the crust different in texture.

LIME CHIFFON PIE

Makes one 9-inch pie.

- 10 to 12 (2½-inch) oatmeal cookies
- ¼ cup (½ stick) butter or margarine
- 2 tablespoons wheat germ
- 1 envelope unflavored gelatin
- ½ cup sugar
- 4 eggs, separated
- 2 tablespoons honey
- ¾ cup milk
- 1 can (6 ounces) frozen limeade concentrate
- Green food coloring
- ½ cup heavy cream

1. Crush cookies in a plastic bag with rolling pin. Melt butter in a medium-size heavy skillet; stir in cookie crumbs and wheat germ; stir over medium heat 1 minute. Press crumb mixture against side and bottom of a 9-inch pie plate. Chill while preparing filling.
2. Mix gelatin and ¼ cup of the sugar in a medium-size saucepan; add egg yolks and honey; beat with a wooden spoon until well blended; gradually stir in milk.
3. Cook, stirring constantly, over medium heat 8 to 10 minutes or until gelatin is completely dissolved and mixture is slightly thickened and coats a spoon. Remove from heat. Stir in limeade concentrate and tint green with a few drops of food coloring. Place pan in bowl of ice and water to speed setting; chill, stirring often, until mixture starts to thicken and mounds when spooned.
4. While lime mixture chills, beat egg whites in a medium-size bowl until foamy-white; gradually beat in remaining ¼ cup sugar until meringue stands in soft peaks. Beat cream in small bowl until stiff.
5. Fold whipped cream, then meringue, into gelatin mixture until no streaks of white remain. Spoon into the chilled piecrust, mounding high. Chill 4 hours or until firm.
6. Garnish with lime slices and sprigs of mint, if you wish.

PEPPERMINT CHIFFON PIE

Makes one 9-inch pie.

- 14 chocolate sandwich cookies
- 3 tablespoons butter or margarine
- 1 envelope unflavored gelatin
- 1 cup milk
- ¾ cup finely crushed peppermint hard candy
- 4 egg whites
- 2 tablespoons sugar
- 1 cup heavy cream, whipped

1. Crush cookies in plastic bag with rolling pin. (Makes about 1¼ cups.) If fillings from cookies stick to inside of bag, scrape off with rubber spatula and blend with crumbs. Melt butter in medium-size skillet; stir in cookie crumbs; remove from heat and stir 1 minute. Press crumb mixture against side and bottom of 9-inch pie plate. Chill while preparing filling.
2. Sprinkle gelatin over milk in small heavy saucepan; let stand a few minutes to soften. Add ½ cup of the crushed candy. Cook, stirring constantly, over medium heat until gelatin is completely dissolved. Place pan in bowl of ice and water to speed setting; chill, stirring often, until mixture starts to thicken.
3. While gelatin mixture chills, beat egg whites in medium-size bowl until foamy-white; gradually beat in sugar until meringue stands in soft peaks.
4. Fold whipped cream, 2 tablespoons of reserved crushed candy and meringue into gelatin mixture until no streaks of white remain; spoon into chilled piecrust. Chill 4 hours or until firm.
5. Just before serving, sprinkle remaining reserved candy over top and decorate with additional whipped cream, if you wish.

DEEP-DISH APPLE PIE

A deep layer of juicy, lightly spiced apples topped with a golden-crisp pastry crust.

Bake at 425° for 45 minutes.
Makes one 10-inch pie.

- 10 medium-size apples (McIntosh, Granny Smith), pared, quartered, cored and sliced (10 cups)
- ⅓ cup firmly packed light brown sugar
- ⅓ cup granulated sugar
- 3 tablespoons flour
- 1 teaspoon ground cinnamon
- ¼ teaspoon ground cloves
- ¼ teaspoon ground allspice
- 1 package piecrust mix
- 2 tablespoons butter or margarine
  Water
- 1 tablespoon granulated sugar

1. Combine apples, brown sugar, the ⅓ cup granulated sugar, flour, cinnamon, cloves and allspice in a large bowl; toss lightly to mix. Let stand while making pastry.
2. Prepare piecrust mix following label directions. Roll out on a lightly floured surface to a 12-inch round. Cut several slits near center to let steam escape.
3. Preheat oven to 425°. Spoon apple mixture into a 10-inch deep pie plate; dot with butter. Cover with pastry; fold edges under, flush with sides of dish. (Pastry should be inside dish.) Pinch to make a stand-up edge; flute. Brush lightly with water; sprinkle with remaining 1 tablespoon of sugar.
4. Bake in a preheated hot oven (425°) for 45 minutes or until pastry is golden and juices bubble up. (Place a piece of aluminum foil on rack under pie to catch any juices that may run over.) Cool at least 1 hour. Serve in individual bowls; pass sour cream, or serve with softened vanilla ice cream.

CHOCOLATE MOUSSE PIE

A unique pie that uses part of the mixture to form its shell.

Bake at 350° for 25 minutes.
Makes one 9-inch pie.

- Packaged bread crumbs
- 8 squares semisweet chocolate
- ¼ cup boiling water
- 8 eggs, separated (whites should be at room temperature)
- ⅔ cup sugar
- 1 teaspoon vanilla
- ⅛ teaspoon salt
- ½ cup cherry preserves
- 1 cup heavy cream, whipped

1. Grease a 9-inch pie plate; dust with bread crumbs.
2. Place chocolate in top of double boiler over hot, not boiling, water. Add boiling water. Cook over low heat, stirring occasionally, until chocolate is almost melted. Remove from heat and continue to stir until smooth. Cool slightly.
3. Beat egg yolks in small bowl with electric mixer at high speed until thick and pale lemon-colored, about 5 minutes. Gradually add sugar; continue beating 5 minutes longer until very thick. Blend in vanilla and chocolate.
4. Preheat oven to 350°. Beat egg whites and salt in large bowl with clean beaters until stiff but not dry. Gradually fold half the whites into chocolate mixture, then fold chocolate into remaining whites, folding only until no streaks of white remain. Spoon part of mousse mixture into prepared pie plate so it just comes level with edge of plate.
5. Bake in a preheated moderate oven (350°) for 25 minutes. Turn off oven heat and leave pie in oven 5 minutes longer. Remove and cool on wire rack 2 hours. As pie cools, mixture will form a shell.
6. Cover and refrigerate remaining uncooked mousse. When the shell has cooled completely, spread cherry preserves over bottom; fill with chilled mousse; chill 2 to 3 hours. Pipe cream through pastry bag around edge. Garnish with chocolate curls and maraschino cherries, if you wish.

———— •◖• ————

PILAF Rice or bulgur (cracked wheat) cooked in a savory broth, often with small bits of meat or vegetables, herbs and spices.

PILAF

Makes 6 servings.

- 1 large onion, diced (1 cup)
- 1 clove garlic, minced
- ¼ cup (½ stick) butter or margarine
- 2 cups chicken broth
- 1 cup uncooked long-grain rice
- ½ cup chopped fresh parsley
- ¼ cup blanched raisins or currants
- ¼ cup pine nuts (pignoli)
  Salt and pepper

1. Sauté onion and garlic in butter in a large saucepan until onion is golden.
2. Add chicken broth. Bring to boiling; stir in rice with a fork; cover; lower heat; cook until rice is tender and all liquid is absorbed.
3. Stir in parsley, raisins and pine nuts. Season with salt and pepper to taste.

———— •◖• ————

PIMIENTO The Spanish word for a sweet, mild red pepper. Fresh pimiento is sometimes available in local produce markets at the end of the summer but most pimientos are preserved in small jars. Fresh pimiento looks like a small, heart-shaped, fleshy red pepper.

PINEAPPLE A tropical fruit, pineapple was so named because it resembled a pine cone. A pineapple which weighs about 4 pounds takes almost 2 years to grow. The pineapple plant is grown from slips or crowns, not seeds. Smooth Cayenne is the leading variety of pineapple grown in Hawaii, Honduras, Mexico, Dominican Republic, the Philippines, Thailand and Costa Rica.

Pineapple is popular for desserts, salads and as an accompaniment to pork and ham. It is a good source of vitamin C with only 52 calories per 3½-ounce serving.

Buying and Storing: Pineapple is available fresh or canned. Fresh pineapples are marketed year-round with peak supplies between April and June. A pineapple does not ripen after it is harvested. Select a pineapple

that is firm with fresh looking green crown leaves. The larger the fruit, the greater the proportion of edible flesh; and it's also a better buy because a pineapple is usually sold by the piece rather than weight. A very slight separation of the eyes and the presence of a fragrance are signs of ripeness. Keep pineapple at room temperature, away from heat or sun; use within 3 days. Refrigerate just until cold before serving.

Canned pineapple is available in slices, chunks and crushed, packed either in juice or sugar syrup.

To Prepare and Serve: Cut off green leaves of fresh pineapple. Cut off rind, removing the eyes. Cut into spears or slices and remove core. For a shell, cut pineapple in half through leaves. Remove flesh from shell using a grapefruit knife. Core flesh and cut into chunks or pieces and refill shells. Or cut pineapple into 4 to 6 wedges through the leaves. Remove flesh from rind; core and cut flesh into crosswise slices and replace on shell. Serve as an appetizer or a refreshing dessert.

Pineapple Tidbit: Do not add *fresh* pineapple to gelatin because it contains an enzyme (bromelain) that will prevent the gelatin from gelling. Because bromelain is deactivated by heat, canned or cooked pineapple can be used in gelatin.

MINT-PINEAPPLE LEMON SHERBET

Fragrant fresh pineapple makes a natural container for refreshing sherbets.

Makes 8 servings.

- **2 pints lemon sherbet**
- **2 tablespoons green crème de menthe**
- **1 fresh pineapple**

1. Spoon 1 pint sherbet into a chilled medium-size bowl; beat until smooth but not melted. Stir in creme de menthe. Spoon back into sherbet container; refreeze overnight or until firm.
2. Cut pineapple in half through top. Carefully cut flesh away from rind, leaving a shell about ½-inch thick. Wrap and refrigerate shells. Remove core from pineapple. Puree about half of the pineapple in an electric blender or food processor to make 1 cup. Slice remaining pineapple thinly; refrigerate.
3. Spoon remaining pint of sherbet into chilled medium-size bowl; beat until soft but not melted; stir in puréed pineapple. Spoon into 3-cup freezer container. Freeze overnight or until firm.
4. To serve: Arrange scoops of mint and pineapple sherbets and sliced pineapple in chilled pineapple shells. Garnish with fresh mint, if you wish.

PINEAPPLE COCONUT CHEESECAKE

A delicious no-bake dessert.

Makes 16 servings.

- **2 packages (8 ounces each) cream cheese**
- **2 cans (8 ounces each) crushed pineapple in pineapple juice**
- **3 teaspoons unflavored gelatin (1½ envelopes)**
- **3 eggs, separated**
- **1 can (15½ ounces) cream of coconut**
- **1 cup zwieback cracker crumbs**
- **½ cup flaked coconut**
- **¼ cup (½ stick) butter or margarine, melted**
- **2 tablespoons sugar**

1. Let the cream cheese soften to room temperature in a large bowl.
2. Drain juice from pineapple into a glass measure; reserve ¾ cup drained pineapple juice and the crushed pineapple.
3. Sprinkle gelatin over pineapple juice in a medium-size saucepan; let stand 5 minutes to soften. Beat egg yolks slightly in a small bowl; stir in cream of coconut, then add mixture to gelatin. Cook over medium heat, stirring constantly, just until mixture comes to boiling, but do not allow to boil. Cool.
4. Combine zwieback crumbs, flaked coconut and butter in a medium-size bowl. Sprinkle ¼ cup mixture around sides of a lightly buttered 9-inch springform pan; press remaining mixture onto bottom. Chill briefly before filling.

5. Beat cream cheese just until smooth with electric mixer at medium speed. Beat in the cooled gelatin mixture.
6. Place pan in a bowl of ice and water to speed set; chill, stirring often, until mixture mounds lightly when dropped from a spoon.
7. While gelatin mixture chills, beat egg whites in small bowl with electric mixer until foamy; slowly beat in sugar until meringue stands in firm peaks.
8. Fold meringue and crushed pineapple into chilled gelatin mixture. Turn into prepared pan. Chill several hours, preferably overnight, until firm. Loosen cake around side with a spatula, then release and remove side.

PINEAPPLE SPEARS IN RUM

Serve these citrus- and rum-flavored spears as stirrers in your next rum-flavored beverage or add to a fruit compote.

Makes 4 pints.

- **2 large ripe pineapples**
- **1 cup sugar**
- **2 cups water**
- **4 thin slices orange**
- **4 thin slices lemon**
- **¼ cup light rum**

1. Cut off leafy crown from pineapple; cut off rind; quarter lengthwise; cut out core; cut each quarter into 4 equal spears. Trim spears, if necessary, to fit wide-mouth pint jars.
2. Combine sugar, water, orange and lemon slices in a large saucepan; bring to boiling; carefully add pineapple spears; bring back to boiling; simmer 5 minutes.
3. Remove spears and place 8 spears and orange and lemon slices into 4 hot sterilized, wide-mouth 16-ounce jars.
4. Drain any syrup that may be in the bottom of the jars back into the saucepan. Boil syrup until reduced to about 1½ cups.
5. Add 1 tablespoon rum to each jar of pineapple spears. Pour in the syrup, leaving ¼-inch head space. Seal; cool; label; date. Store in refrigerator.

Pictured opposite: Mint-Pineapple Lemon Sherbet, page 507

Overleaf: Sausage and Pepper Pizza, page 512; (Insets from top) South-of-the-Border Pizza, page 512; Pizza Rustica, page 512; Pizza, Mariner's Style, page 511

Pineapple

PINEAPPLE PIE

Bake at 425° for 35 minutes.
Makes one 9-inch pie.

- **1 package piecrust mix**
- **1 teaspoon grated lemon rind**
- **¾ cup sugar**
- **3 tablespoons cornstarch**
- **1 can (20 ounces) crushed pineapple in pineapple juice**
- **1 tablespoon lemon juice**

1. Prepare piecrust mix following label directions for a two-crust pie, adding the lemon rind with the liquid called for in the directions.
2. Roll out half the pastry to a 12-inch round on a lightly floured pastry board. Fit into a 9-inch pie plate. Trim overhang to ½ inch.
3. Combine sugar, cornstarch, pineapple with its juice and lemon juice in a medium-size saucepan. Cook over medium heat, stirring constantly, until mixture thickens and boils 1 minute. Remove from heat. Cool slightly. Pour into pastry-lined pie plate.
4. Preheat oven to 425°. Roll out remaining pastry to an 11-inch round; cut vents in center to allow steam to escape during baking. Place over filling; pinch edges to seal. Pinch to make a stand-up edge; flute. Brush crust with milk and sprinkle with sugar, if you wish.
5. Bake in a preheated hot oven (425°) for 35 minutes or until pie is golden brown. Cool on wire rack.

COOL CUCUMBER-PINEAPPLE MOLD

Makes 8 servings.

- **2 medium-size cucumbers**
- **1 can (20 ounces) crushed pineapple in pineapple juice**
- **1 package (6 ounces) lime-flavored gelatin**
- **2 cups boiling water**
- **¼ cup cider vinegar**
- **½ cup mayonnaise**
- **½ cup dairy sour cream**
- **2 teaspoons salt**
- **½ teaspoon dillweed**

1. Pare cucumbers; halve; remove seeds. Shred on smallest side of food shredder; drain thoroughly, pressing out as much liquid as possible.
2. Drain juice from pineapple into a 1-cup liquid measure. Add water to make 1 cup liquid. Reserve.
3. Dissolve gelatin in boiling water in a medium-size bowl. Stir in reserved pineapple juice and vinegar. Place bowl in a pan of ice and water to speed setting. Chill, stirring often, until as thick as unbeaten egg white.
4. Stir in cucumbers, pineapple, mayonnaise, sour cream, salt and dillweed.
5. Continue to chill over ice and water until mixture again becomes as thick as unbeaten egg white.
6. Pour into an 8-cup mold. Chill until firm, about 4 hours. To unmold: Run a thin-bladed knife around top edge of mold. Dip mold very quickly in and out of hot water. Invert serving plate over top of mold; turn plate upright with mold; shake gently to loosen; lift off. Refrigerate until ready to serve. Garnish with lettuce or chicory, if you wish.

— ●●● —

PINE NUTS The edible seeds of the cones of a variety of pine tree which grow in the mountainous states of the Southwest. Pine nuts are also called Indian nuts, pignons or piñons. In Italy and France pine nuts are called *pinoleas* or *pignolias*. American-grown pine nuts are smaller than the European nuts.

Pine nuts are ivory-colored, sweet-tasting kernels. They are sold unshelled or shelled, always raw or unroasted.

Pine Nut Nutrition: An ounce of pine nuts has 158 calories and 8 grams of protein.

PINE NUT MACAROONS

Lacy and sugary, with nut-covered tops, and so easy to make.

Bake at 375° for 10 minutes.
Makes about 2½ dozen cookies.

- **1 cup blanched almonds**
- **1 cup sugar**
- **2 egg whites**
- **½ teaspoon almond extract**
- **1 jar (8 ounces) pine nuts (pignolias)**

1. Dry blanched almonds thoroughly by placing them in a warm oven (350°) for 5 to 10 minutes. Grind as fine as possible in an electric blender or food processor until powdery, while still warm.
2. Combine ground almonds and sugar in a medium-size bowl; add unbeaten egg whites and almond extract; beat thoroughly.
3. Drop by teaspoonfuls onto generously buttered and floured cookie sheets, leaving 1 inch between cookies. Smooth into rounds. Top each cookie with approximately ½ teaspoon pine nuts, pressing pine nuts into cookie. Let stand 3 hours.
4. Bake in a preheated moderate oven (375°) for 10 minutes. Remove cookies from oven; let stand on cookie sheets for 5 minutes; carefully remove with wide spatula (if cookies stiffen, put back into oven for a few seconds to soften). Store in airtight container when thoroughly cooled.

— ●●● —

PINK BEANS Used similarly to pinto beans in Mexican cooking, pink beans are pinkish-tan with no mottling. See also **BEANS**.

PINTO BEANS Medium-size, pale pink beans mottled with brown, used extensively in Tex-Mex and Mexican cooking. These are all-purpose beans which turn a solid reddish-brown when cooked. They are good in soups, salads and casseroles. See also **BEANS**.

PINTO BEAN SALAD

Makes 6 servings.

- **1 cup dried pinto beans (½ pound)**
- **4 cups water**
- **2 cups torn fresh spinach leaves, loosely packed**
- **1 cup sliced zucchini (1 small)**
- **1 cup sliced fennel**
- **4 ounces Swiss cheese, cubed Tangy Mustard Dressing (recipe follows)**

1. Pick over beans and rinse under running water. Combine beans and 4 cups cold water in a large kettle. Bring to boiling; cover; simmer 1½ hours

or until beans are firm-tender. Drain; chill several hours.

2. To serve: Arrange spinach, zucchini, fennel, Swiss cheese and beans in a large salad bowl. Pour dressing over all; toss to coat evenly.

Tangy Mustard Dressing: Combine ¾ cup mayonnaise or salad dressing, 2 tablespoons vinegar, 1 tablespoon lemon juice, 2 tablespoons grated onion, 1 tablespoon Dijon mustard, ½ teaspoon salt, ¼ teaspoon cracked black pepper in a small bowl. Refrigerate, covered, at least 1 hour. Makes 1 cup.

PINTO BEANS

Makes 4 to 6 servings.

- 1 pound dried pinto beans
- 5 cups water
- 1 medium-size onion, chopped (½ cup)
- 1 clove garlic, minced
- 1 teaspoon chili powder
- ¼ pound salt pork, cut into ¼-inch cubes
- 1 teaspoon salt

1. Pick over beans and rinse under running water. Combine beans and enough water to cover in a large kettle; cover; let soak overnight. Or, to quick-soak, bring to boiling; boil 2 minutes; remove from heat. Cover and let stand 1 hour. Drain.

2. Add the 5 cups water, onion, garlic, chili powder and salt pork to beans. Bring to boiling; lower heat; simmer over low heat 2½ hours or until beans are tender. (If beans appear dry, add more water to moisten.) Stir in salt.

REFRIED BEANS

Makes 3 cups.

- 1 recipe Pinto Beans *(recipe above)*
- ½ cup bacon drippings or lard
- 2 ounces Longhorn or mild Cheddar cheese, shredded (½ cup)

1. Drain beans and mash in a bowl.

2. Heat drippings in a large skillet over medium heat. Add beans; cook, stirring constantly, until beans are thick and fat has been absorbed. Serve topped with shredded cheese.

MEXICAN BEAN POT

Bake at 325° for 2 hours.
Makes 6 servings.

- 1 pound dried pinto beans
- 6 cups water
- ½ pound hot Italian sausage
- 1 large onion, chopped (1 cup)
- 2 large green peppers, halved, seeded and cut into large pieces
- 2 to 4 teaspoons chili powder
- 2 teaspoons salt
- 1 teaspoon leaf basil, crumbled
- 2 envelopes or teaspoons instant beef broth

1. Pick over beans and wash; place in a large saucepan and add water; bring to boiling; lower heat; cover saucepan; simmer 1 hour.

2. While beans cook, cut sausage into small pieces; brown in a small skillet; remove with slotted spoon and reserve. Sauté onion until soft; stir in peppers and sauté 2 minutes longer; add chili powder, salt, basil and instant beef broth; cook, stirring constantly, 2 minutes.

3. Transfer cooked beans to a 10-cup casserole with a slotted spoon; reserve cooking liquid; add sausage pieces and sautéed vegetables to cooked beans and mix until well blended. Add enough bean cooking liquid to cover beans.

4. Bake in a slow oven (325°) for 2 hours or until beans are tender and liquid thickens. (If the beans seem too dry, add more cooking liquid.)

———— •●• ————

PISTACHIO The pistachio is the stone or seed of the fruit of the pistachio tree. The fruit is red, about ½ inch long, and grows in bunches. A pistachio nut has a double shell. The red outer shell is removed; the inside shell is grayish-white, thin, smooth, and brittle. Pistachio nuts are often dyed red to make the shell a uniform color.

The greenish seeds or nuts are used as snacks, for desserts and candy.

Pistachio nuts are available unshelled and sometimes shelled. Until recently, most were imported from Turkey but some are now grown in California.

Pistachio Nutrition: An ounce contains 170 calories and 5.5 grams of protein.

PITA BREAD A flat, round, soft bread which originated in the Middle East. Also called Syrian or pocket bread. After baking, the bread forms 2 layers or a pocket. Pita can be filled with meat, cheese or vegetables, or split, buttered and toasted.

PIZZA The Italian word for pie. Pizza has become a popular American snack food. It can be made from any number of ingredients.

PIZZA, MARINER'S STYLE

Bake at 450° for 15 to 20 minutes.
Makes two 12-inch pizzas.

- 1 loaf (1 pound) frozen plain bread dough, thawed overnight in refrigerator
- 1 jar (15½ ounces) thick Italian-style cooking sauce
- 1 can (7 ounces) tuna, drained
- 1 can (5¾ ounces) pitted ripe olives
- 2 jars (2½ ounces each) whole mushrooms, drained
- 2 jars (6 ounces each) marinated artichoke hearts, drained
- 1 package (8 ounces) mozzarella cheese, finely diced
- 2 cans (2 ounces each) rolled anchovy filets, drained
  Parsley sprigs

1. Divide dough in half; stretch to fit two lightly oiled 12-inch pizza pans, pressing against bottoms and sides of pans, keeping dough slightly thicker on edges. Allow crusts to rest 10 to 15 minutes.

2. Preheat oven to 450°. Spread half of sauce on each pizza. Break up tuna; divide between pizzas. Alternate olives and mushrooms around edge; arrange artichokes on pizza; top with cheese.

3. Bake in a preheated very hot oven (450°) for 15 to 20 minutes or until crusts are golden. Garnish with anchovy and parsley.

Pizza

PIZZA RUSTICA

Bake at 350° for 50 minutes.
Makes one 12-inch double-crust pizza.

- **1 package hot roll mix**
  OR: Easy Pizza Dough (recipe follows)
- **¾ cup plus 2 tablespoons very warm water**
- **1 container (15 ounces) ricotta cheese**
- **1 package (8 ounces) mozzarella cheese, shredded**
- **¼ pound salami, finely diced**
- **⅓ cup sliced green onions**
- **3 tablespoons chopped fresh parsley**
- **1 teaspoon leaf oregano, crumbled**
- **1 teaspoon salt**
- **3 eggs, slightly beaten**

1. Sprinkle yeast from hot roll mix into very warm water in medium-size bowl; stir until dissolved. ("Very warm water" should feel comfortably warm when dropped on wrist.) Gradually work in flour of hot roll mix to form a fairly stiff dough. Place dough in an oiled bowl; cover. Let rise in warm place until double in volume, about 30 minutes.

2. Meanwhile, prepare filling: Combine ricotta, mozzarella, salami, green onions, parsley, oregano, salt and eggs, reserving about 2 tablespoons of the beaten egg for brushing.

3. Preheat oven to 350°. Punch dough down and divide in half. Lightly oil a 12-inch pizza pan. Stretch one half of dough to fit pan, pressing dough against side of pan to make an edge. Brush edge with reserved beaten egg. Spoon filling over dough. Roll remaining half of dough to a 12-inch round; fit over filling, pressing edges together. Prick entire surface with a two-tined fork. Cut decorations from trimmings. Brush top with egg. Decorate top. Brush decorations.

4. Bake in a preheated moderate oven (350°) for 50 minutes or until golden brown. Cover top with foil if pizza is browning too fast. Let stand 15 minutes before cutting into wedges to serve.

EASY PIZZA DOUGH

Makes one thick 14-inch round crust or two thin 12-inch round crusts.

- **1 package active dry yeast**
- **½ teaspoon sugar**
- **1 cup very warm water**
- **3¼ cups *sifted* all-purpose flour**
- **1½ teaspoons salt**

1. Sprinkle yeast and sugar into very warm water in a 1-cup measure. ("Very warm water" should feel comfortably warm when dropped on wrist.) Stir to dissolve and allow to stand 10 minutes or until mixture begins to bubble.

2. Combine flour and salt in a large bowl; make a well in the center; pour in yeast mixture; gradually work in flour to form a stiff dough.

3. Turn out onto lightly floured surface. Knead until smooth and elastic, about 5 minutes, using only as much flour as necessary to keep dough from sticking.

4. Place in lightly oiled medium-size bowl; turn dough to coat all over with oil. Cover with clean towel. Let rise in a warm place away from drafts 45 minutes or until double in volume. Punch down and use as directed.

SOUTH-OF-THE-BORDER PIZZA

Bake at 450° for 15 minutes.
Makes one 12-inch pizza.

- **¾ pound ground chuck**
- **1 can (7½ ounces) taco sauce**
- **1¼ cups buttermilk baking mix**
- **½ cup yellow cornmeal**
- **½ cup milk**
- **1 can (4 ounces) whole mild green chilies, drained and cut into strips**
- **1 package (8 ounces) natural Monterey Jack cheese slices**
  Sliced green onion
  Shredded lettuce
  Pickled red cherry peppers

1. Brown meat lightly in large skillet; stir in taco sauce; cook, uncovered, 5 minutes or until almost dry. Remove from heat. Cool.

2. Preheat oven to 450°. Combine baking mix and cornmeal in a large bowl; add milk; mix with a fork until moistened; press, with floured hands, on lightly greased cookie sheet to a 12-inch round. Spread meat mixture over dough to edge. Arrange chilies and cheese over meat.

3. Bake in a preheated very hot oven (450°) for 15 minutes or until edges are brown and cheese is melted. Sprinkle with green onions and shredded lettuce; garnish with pickled red cherry peppers.

SAUSAGE AND PEPPER PIZZA

Bake at 450° for 25 minutes.
Makes one 14-inch pizza.

- **Cornmeal**
  Easy Pizza Dough (recipe, this page)
- **½ pound sweet Italian sausages**
- **1 can (15 ounces) tomato sauce with tomato bits**
- **¼ cup grated Parmesan cheese**
- **1 green pepper, halved, seeded and cut into strips**
- **1 red pepper, halved, seeded and cut into strips**
- **2 small onions, sliced**
- **1 package (8 ounces) mozzarella cheese, shredded**

1. Lightly oil a 14-inch round pizza pan; sprinkle lightly with cornmeal. Roll and stretch pizza dough to fit pan. Let rise 20 minutes.

2. Preheat oven to 450°. Remove sausage from casings; sauté meat in large skillet until no longer pink. Add tomato sauce; cook, stirring often, until juices have evaporated and mixture is almost dry, about 5 minutes. Remove from heat; cool slightly. Spread meat mixture over dough; sprinkle with Parmesan cheese.

3. Bake in a preheated very hot oven (450°) for 10 minutes; remove from oven. Arrange peppers and onions over top; sprinkle with cheese. Return to oven. Bake 15 to 20 minutes longer or until crust is golden brown and cheese is melted and bubbly. Cut into wedges to serve.

●●●